CALIFORNIA
GUIDE TO THE ESSENTIALS
OF

American
Government

PEARSON

Prentice
Hall

Boston, Massachusetts

Upper Saddle River, New Jersey

TO THE TEACHER

The *Guide to the Essentials of American Government* is designed to provide students with the most essential content in their high school government or civics course in an easy-to-follow format. The text summaries and graphic organizers will help students organize key information. Vocabulary terms are highlighted and defined in the text narrative, as well as in the glossary. A chapter test at the end of each chapter checks students' understanding of the basic content.

You may wish to use the *Guide to the Essentials* as a preview or review of the textbook chapters covered in the course, or as a summary of textbook chapters that cannot be studied in detail because of time considerations.

Consultants
William A. McClenaghan
Department of Political Science
Oregon State University
Corvallis, Oregon

Bonnie Armbruster
Professor of Education
University of Illinois at Urbana-Champaign
Urbana, Illinois

Development
Prentice Hall and
Publicom, Inc.
Acton, Massachusetts

PEARSON
Prentice
Hall

ISBN 0-13-251361-7
13 14 15   V016   14 13 12 11

Contents

The Judicial Branch

Comparative Political and Economic Systems

Participating in California State and Local Government

GOVERNMENT DATA BANK

Three Branches of U.S. Government

LEGISLATIVE

Senate
House of Representatives

Makes laws

Overrides presidential vetoes

Approves presidential appointments

Approves treaties

Taxes to provide services

Provides for defense, declares war

Regulates money and trade

Impeaches officials

EXECUTIVE

President
Vice President

Enforces laws and treaties

Can veto laws

Appoints high officials

Conducts foreign policy

Enforces laws and treaties

Commander in chief of the military

Recommends bills to Congress

Reports the state of the
Union to Congress

JUDICIAL

Supreme Court
Federal Courts

Explains and interprets laws

Settles legal disputes between states

Settles State and federal disputes

Settles disputes between States
and foreign countries

Hears cases with ambassadors
of foreign governments

Settles disputes between individuals
and Federal Government

Source: U.S. Department of Justice

Federalism

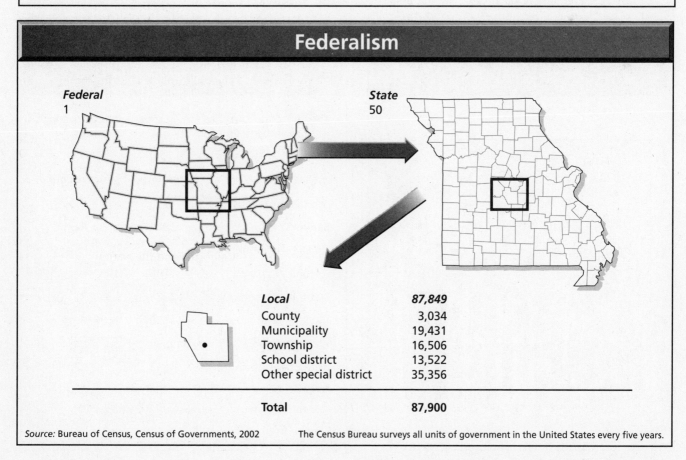

Federal
1

State
50

Local	87,849
County	3,034
Municipality	19,431
Township	16,506
School district	13,522
Other special district	35,356
Total	**87,900**

Source: Bureau of Census, Census of Governments, 2002   The Census Bureau surveys all units of government in the United States every five years.

How the Federal Government Uses Your Tax Dollar

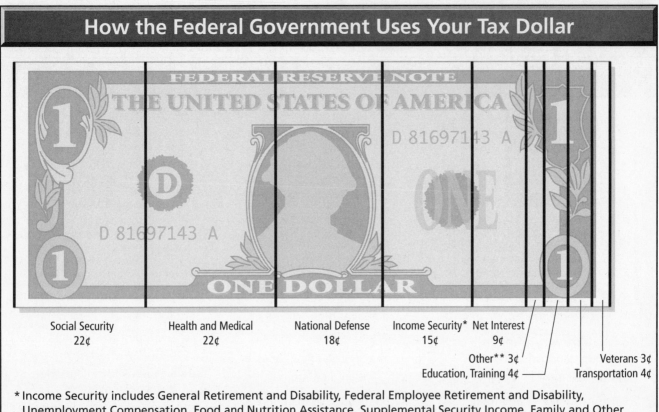

Social Security 22¢	Health and Medical 22¢	National Defense 18¢	Income Security* 15¢	Net Interest 9¢

Other** 3¢

Education, Training 4¢

Veterans 3¢

Transportation 4¢

* Income Security includes General Retirement and Disability, Federal Employee Retirement and Disability, Unemployment Compensation, Food and Nutrition Assistance, Supplemental Security Income, Family and Other Support Assistance, Earned Income Tax Credit, Offsetting Receipts, and Housing Assistance.

** Other includes Energy, Natural Resources and Environment, Commerce and Housing Credit, Community and Regional Development, International Affairs, General Science, Space and Technology, Agriculture, Administration of Justice, General Government Allowances, and Undistributed Offsetting Receipts.

Source: The Tax Foundation (2003 data)

History of the Minimum Wage

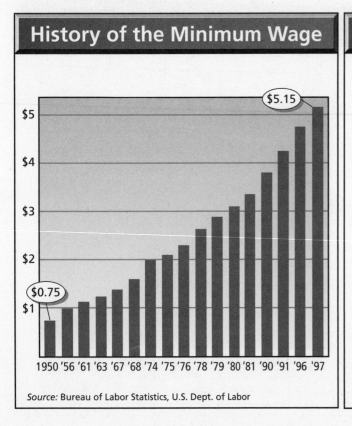

$5.15

$0.75

1950 '56 '61 '63 '67 '68 '74 '75 '76 '78 '79 '80 '81 '90 '91 '96 '97

Source: Bureau of Labor Statistics, U.S. Dept. of Labor

Supreme Court

The Supreme Court has nine justices: eight associate justices and one Chief Justice. All are appointed by the President and confirmed by the Senate.

Justice	Appointed	President
John Paul Stevens	1975	Ford
Sandra Day O'Connor	1981	Reagan
William H. Rehnquist*	1986	Reagan
Antonin Scalia	1986	Reagan
Anthony M. Kennedy	1988	Reagan
David H. Souter	1990	Bush
Clarence Thomas	1991	Bush
Ruth Bader Ginsburg	1993	Clinton
Stephen Breyer	1994	Clinton

* Chief Justice; appointed as an associate justice by President Nixon in 1971.

Source: The U.S. Government Manual

The U.S. Government

Legislative

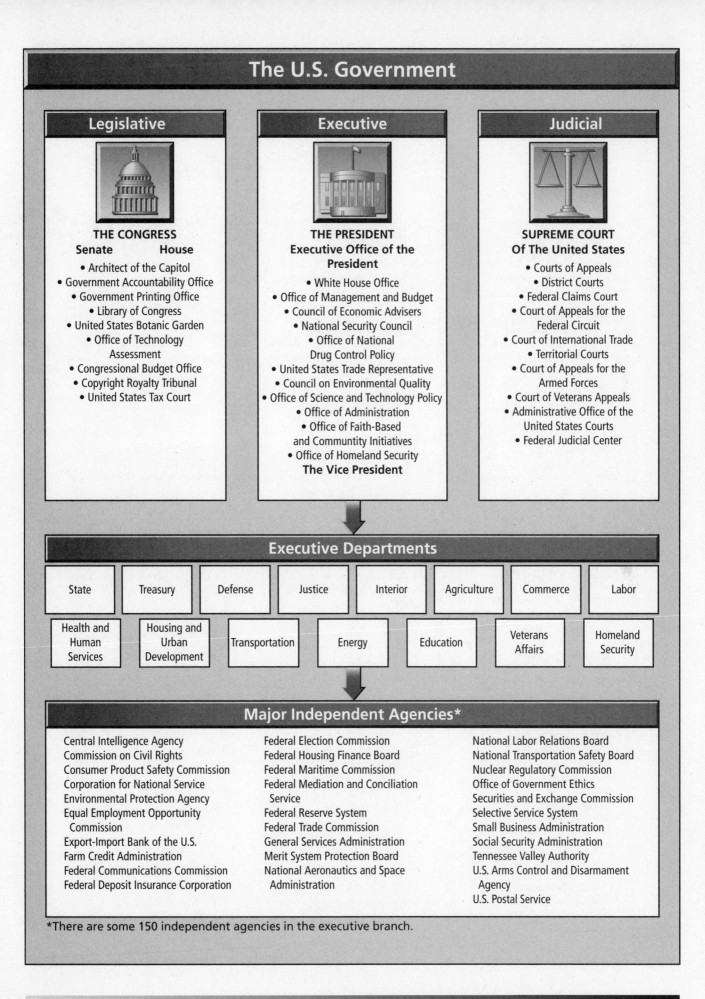

THE CONGRESS
Senate   House

- Architect of the Capitol
- Government Accountability Office
- Government Printing Office
- Library of Congress
- United States Botanic Garden
- Office of Technology Assessment
- Congressional Budget Office
- Copyright Royalty Tribunal
- United States Tax Court

Executive

THE PRESIDENT
Executive Office of the President

- White House Office
- Office of Management and Budget
- Council of Economic Advisers
- National Security Council
- Office of National Drug Control Policy
- United States Trade Representative
- Council on Environmental Quality
- Office of Science and Technology Policy
- Office of Administration
- Office of Faith-Based and Communtity Initiatives
- Office of Homeland Security

The Vice President

Judicial

SUPREME COURT
Of The United States

- Courts of Appeals
- District Courts
- Federal Claims Court
- Court of Appeals for the Federal Circuit
- Court of International Trade
- Territorial Courts
- Court of Appeals for the Armed Forces
- Court of Veterans Appeals
- Administrative Office of the United States Courts
- Federal Judicial Center

Executive Departments

State	Treasury	Defense	Justice	Interior	Agriculture	Commerce	Labor
Health and Human Services	Housing and Urban Development	Transportation	Energy	Education	Veterans Affairs	Homeland Security

Major Independent Agencies*

Central Intelligence Agency
Commission on Civil Rights
Consumer Product Safety Commission
Corporation for National Service
Environmental Protection Agency
Equal Employment Opportunity Commission
Export-Import Bank of the U.S.
Farm Credit Administration
Federal Communications Commission
Federal Deposit Insurance Corporation

Federal Election Commission
Federal Housing Finance Board
Federal Maritime Commission
Federal Mediation and Conciliation Service
Federal Reserve System
Federal Trade Commission
General Services Administration
Merit System Protection Board
National Aeronautics and Space Administration

National Labor Relations Board
National Transportation Safety Board
Nuclear Regulatory Commission
Office of Government Ethics
Securities and Exchange Commission
Selective Service System
Small Business Administration
Social Security Administration
Tennessee Valley Authority
U.S. Arms Control and Disarmament Agency
U.S. Postal Service

*There are some 150 independent agencies in the executive branch.

We the People of the United States, in ord ... nsure domestic Tranquility, provide for the common defence, promote the general Welfare, ... nd our Posterity, do ordain and establish this Constitution for the United States of Amer ...

Amendment 1
Congress may not violate the rights of freedom of religion, speech, press, peaceable assembly, and petition.

Amendment 2
Each state has the right to maintain a militia. Individuals can own and use weapons.

Amendment 3
The government may not quarter, or house, soldiers in the people's homes during peacetime without the people's permission.

Amendment 4
The government may not search or take a person's property without a warrant.

Amendment 5
A person may not be tried twice for the same crime and does not have to testify against him/herself.

Amendment 6
A person charged with a crime has the right to a speedy trial, an impartial jury, and a lawyer.

Amendment 7
A person in a civil case is guaranteed a trial by jury.

Amendment 8
A person is protected from excessive or unreasonable fines or cruel and unusual punishment.

Amendment 9
The people have rights other than those mentioned in the Constitution.

Amendment 10
Any power not given to the Federal Government by the Constitution is a power of either the State or the people.

Amendment 11
Citizens of a State or foreign country may not sue another State in federal court.

Amendment 12
The Electoral College will vote separately for President and Vice President rather than together in one ballot.

Amendment 13
Slavery is outlawed in the United States.

Amendment 14
States shall not deprive persons of life, liberty, or property without due process. The Three-Fifths Compromise is repealed, and all persons are counted in the census.

Amendment 15
Citizens are guaranteed the right to vote, regardless of race, color, or status of former slave.

Amendment 16
Congress has the right to set up an income tax.

Amendment 17
U.S. Senators are elected directly by voters in each State.

Amendment 18
Making or selling alcohol is illegal.

Amendment 19
Citizens are guaranteed the right to vote, regardless of sex.

Amendment 20
The President takes office on January 20, and Congress's term begins January 3.

Amendment 21
This amendment repealed the 18th Amendment.

Amendment 22
No president can be elected to more than two terms.

Amendment 23
People living in Washington, D.C., may vote in presidential and vice presidential election. D.C. has three presidential electors.

Amendment 24
People may vote for President, Vice President, and Congress without paying a voting tax.

Amendment 25
The Vice President becomes the President if the President is disabled.

Amendment 26
Citizens who are at least 18 years of age are guaranteed the right to vote.

Amendment 27
Any pay raise the House of Representatives may approve for its members does not take effect until after the next congressional election.

Who Are the American People?

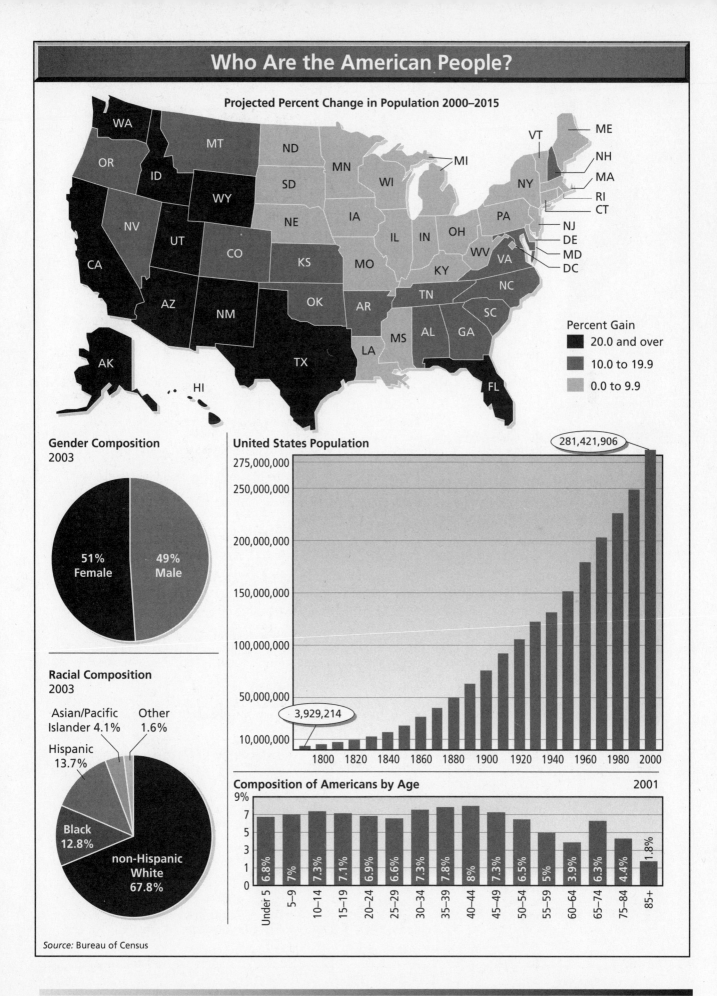

Projected Percent Change in Population 2000–2015

Percent Gain
- 20.0 and over
- 10.0 to 19.9
- 0.0 to 9.9

Gender Composition
2003

- 51% Female
- 49% Male

Racial Composition
2003

- Asian/Pacific Islander 4.1%
- Other 1.6%
- Hispanic 13.7%
- Black 12.8%
- non-Hispanic White 67.8%

United States Population

281,421,906

3,929,214

275,000,000
250,000,000
200,000,000
150,000,000
100,000,000
50,000,000
10,000,000

1800 1820 1840 1860 1880 1900 1920 1940 1960 1980 2000

Composition of Americans by Age
2001

9%
7
5
3
1
0

Age	Percent
Under 5	6.8%
5–9	7%
10–14	7.3%
15–19	7.1%
20–24	6.9%
25–29	6.6%
30–34	7.3%
35–39	7.8%
40–44	8%
45–49	7.3%
50–54	6.5%
55–59	5%
60–64	3.9%
65–74	6.3%
75–84	4.4%
85+	1.8%

Source: Bureau of Census

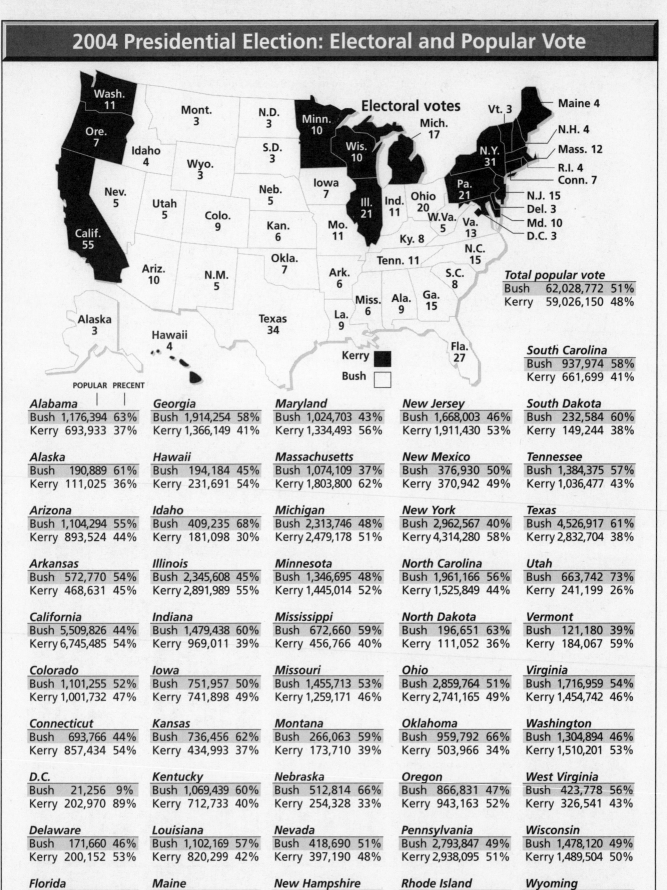

Electoral votes

Wash. 11	Maine 4
Ore. 7	N.H. 4
Mont. 3	Mass. 12
N.D. 3	R.I. 4
Minn. 10	Conn. 7
Mich. 17	N.J. 15
Vt. 3	Del. 3
N.Y. 31	Md. 10
Pa. 21	D.C. 3

Idaho 4, Wyo. 3, S.D. 3, Wis. 10, Iowa 7, Ill. 21, Ind. 11, Ohio 20, W.Va. 5, Va. 13
Nev. 5, Utah 5, Colo. 9, Neb. 5, Mo. 11, Ky. 8, N.C. 15
Calif. 55, Ariz. 10, N.M. 5, Kan. 6, Okla. 7, Ark. 6, Tenn. 11, S.C. 8
Alaska 3, Texas 34, La. 9, Miss. 6, Ala. 9, Ga. 15
Hawaii 4, Fla. 27

Kerry ■
Bush □

Total popular vote

Bush	62,028,772	51%
Kerry	59,026,150	48%

South Carolina

Bush	937,974	58%
Kerry	661,699	41%

POPULAR PRECENT

Alabama

Bush	1,176,394	63%
Kerry	693,933	37%

Alaska

Bush	190,889	61%
Kerry	111,025	36%

Arizona

Bush	1,104,294	55%
Kerry	893,524	44%

Arkansas

Bush	572,770	54%
Kerry	468,631	45%

California

Bush	5,509,826	44%
Kerry	6,745,485	54%

Colorado

Bush	1,101,255	52%
Kerry	1,001,732	47%

Connecticut

Bush	693,766	44%
Kerry	857,434	54%

D.C.

Bush	21,256	9%
Kerry	202,970	89%

Delaware

Bush	171,660	46%
Kerry	200,152	53%

Florida

Bush	3,964,522	52%
Kerry	3,583,544	47%

Georgia

Bush	1,914,254	58%
Kerry	1,366,149	41%

Hawaii

Bush	194,184	45%
Kerry	231,691	54%

Idaho

Bush	409,235	68%
Kerry	181,098	30%

Illinois

Bush	2,345,608	45%
Kerry	2,891,989	55%

Indiana

Bush	1,479,438	60%
Kerry	969,011	39%

Iowa

Bush	751,957	50%
Kerry	741,898	49%

Kansas

Bush	736,456	62%
Kerry	434,993	37%

Kentucky

Bush	1,069,439	60%
Kerry	712,733	40%

Louisiana

Bush	1,102,169	57%
Kerry	820,299	42%

Maine

Bush	330,201	45%
Kerry	396,842	54%

Maryland

Bush	1,024,703	43%
Kerry	1,334,493	56%

Massachusetts

Bush	1,074,109	37%
Kerry	1,803,800	62%

Michigan

Bush	2,313,746	48%
Kerry	2,479,178	51%

Minnesota

Bush	1,346,695	48%
Kerry	1,445,014	52%

Mississippi

Bush	672,660	59%
Kerry	456,766	40%

Missouri

Bush	1,455,713	53%
Kerry	1,259,171	46%

Montana

Bush	266,063	59%
Kerry	173,710	39%

Nebraska

Bush	512,814	66%
Kerry	254,328	33%

Nevada

Bush	418,690	51%
Kerry	397,190	48%

New Hampshire

Bush	331,257	49%
Kerry	340,511	50%

New Jersey

Bush	1,668,003	46%
Kerry	1,911,430	53%

New Mexico

Bush	376,930	50%
Kerry	370,942	49%

New York

Bush	2,962,567	40%
Kerry	4,314,280	58%

North Carolina

Bush	1,961,166	56%
Kerry	1,525,849	44%

North Dakota

Bush	196,651	63%
Kerry	111,052	36%

Ohio

Bush	2,859,764	51%
Kerry	2,741,165	49%

Oklahoma

Bush	959,792	66%
Kerry	503,966	34%

Oregon

Bush	866,831	47%
Kerry	943,163	52%

Pennsylvania

Bush	2,793,847	49%
Kerry	2,938,095	51%

Rhode Island

Bush	169,046	39%
Kerry	259,760	59%

South Dakota

Bush	232,584	60%
Kerry	149,244	38%

Tennessee

Bush	1,384,375	57%
Kerry	1,036,477	43%

Texas

Bush	4,526,917	61%
Kerry	2,832,704	38%

Utah

Bush	663,742	73%
Kerry	241,199	26%

Vermont

Bush	121,180	39%
Kerry	184,067	59%

Virginia

Bush	1,716,959	54%
Kerry	1,454,742	46%

Washington

Bush	1,304,894	46%
Kerry	1,510,201	53%

West Virginia

Bush	423,778	56%
Kerry	326,541	43%

Wisconsin

Bush	1,478,120	49%
Kerry	1,489,504	50%

Wyoming

Bush	167,629	69%
Kerry	70,776	29%

Source: Infoplease

The Political Parties in Congress

Party Strength (at the beginning of term)

House of Representatives — 435 Members

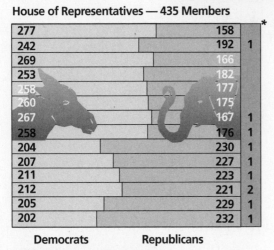

Democrats	Republicans	*	
277	158		1979–81
242	192	1	1981–83
269	166		1983–85
253	182		1985–87
258	177		1987–89
260	175		1989–91
267	167	1	1991–93
258	176	1	1993–95
204	230	1	1995–97
207	227	1	1997–99
211	223	1	1999–2001
212	221	2	2001–2003
205	229	1	2003–2005
202	232	1	2005-2007

Note: Numbers do not always add to 435 (or 100) due to vacancies.

Senate — 100 Members

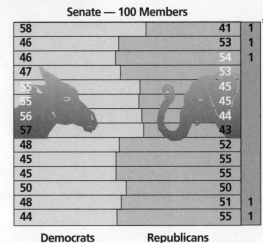

Democrats	Republicans	*
58	41	1
46	53	1
46	54	1
47	53	
55	45	
55	45	
56	44	
57	43	
48	52	
45	55	
45	55	
50	50	
48	51	1
44	55	1

*Independent

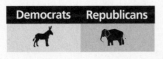

Democrats	Republicans

Representation by State (109th Congress)

	HOUSE (D)	HOUSE (R)	SENATE (D)	SENATE (R)		HOUSE (D)	HOUSE (R)	SENATE (D)	SENATE (R)
Alabama	2	5	0	2	Montana	0	1	1	1
Alaska	0	1	0	2	Nebraska	0	3	1	1
Arizona	2	6	0	2	Nevada	1	2	1	1
Arkansas	3	1	2	0	New Hampshire	0	2	0	2
California	33	20	2	0	New Jersey	7	6	2	0
Colorado	3	4	1	1	New Mexico	1	2	1	1
Connecticut	2	3	2	0	New York	20	9	2	0
Delaware	0	1	2	0	North Carolina	6	7	0	2
Florida	7	18	1	1	North Dakota	1	0	2	0
Georgia	6	7	0	2	Ohio	6	12	0	2
Hawaii	2	0	2	0	Oklahoma	1	4	0	2
Idaho	0	2	0	2	Oregon	4	1	1	1
Illinois	10	9	2	0	Pennsylvania	7	12	0	2
Indiana	2	7	1	1	Rhode Island	2	0	1	1
Iowa	1	4	1	1	South Carolina	2	4	0	2
Kansas	1	3	0	2	South Dakota	1	0	1	1
Kentucky	1	5	0	2	Tennessee	5	4	0	2
Louisiana	2	5	1	1	Texas	11	21	0	2
Maine	2	0	0	2	Utah	1	2	0	2
Maryland	6	2	2	0	Vermont	0 *	0	1 *	0
Massachusetts	10	0	2	0	Virginia	3	8	0	2
Michigan	6	9	2	0	Washington	6	3	2	0
Minnesota	4	4	1	1	West Virginia	2	1	2	0
Mississippi	2	2	0	2	Wisconsin	4	4	2	0
Missouri	4	5	0	2	Wyoming	0	1	0	2

* One Independent

Sources: Clerk of the House, Congressional Quarterly, Washington Post

The Six Basic Principles of Government

The Constitution of the United States is built on six basic principles of government. The Framers of the Constitution drew on their knowledge and experience to craft a document that serves as "the supreme law of the land." The descriptions at the beginning of each unit will help you see how these six principles—and the Constitution itself—have proved an enduring yet flexible guide for governing the nation for over 200 years.

POPULAR SOVEREIGNTY

The Preamble to the Constitution begins with this bold phrase: "We the people . . ." These words announce that in the United States, the people establish government and give it its power. The people are sovereign. Since the government receives its power from the people, it can govern only with their consent.

LIMITED GOVERNMENT

Because the people are the source of government power, the government has only as much authority as the people give it. Much of the Constitution, in fact, consists of specific limitations on government power. Limited government means that neither the government itself nor any government official is "above the law" and can overstep these constitutional bounds.

SEPARATION OF POWERS

Government power is not only limited; it is also divided. The Constitution assigns specific powers to each of the three branches: the legislative (Congress), the executive (President), and the judicial (federal courts). This separation of powers is intended to prevent misuse of power by one branch of government.

CHECKS AND BALANCES

The system of checks and balances extends the restrictions established by the separation of powers. Each branch of government has the built-in authority and responsibility to restrain the power of the other two branches. This system makes government less efficient but also prevents tyranny by one branch of government.

JUDICIAL REVIEW

Who decides whether an act of government oversteps the limits placed on it by the Constitution? Historically, the judges in the federal courts have made the decisions. The principle of judicial review was established early in the history of the nation. It means that federal courts have the power to review government acts and to nullify, or cancel, any that are unconstitutional, or violate a provision of the Constitution.

FEDERALISM

A federal system divides power between a central government and smaller, local governments. This sharing of power is intended to ensure that the central government is powerful enough to be effective, yet not so powerful as to threaten States or citizens. It also allows individual States to deal with local problems at the local level—so long as their actions are constitutional.

Principles of Government

 SECTION 1 — *GOVERNMENT AND THE STATE*

■ TEXT SUMMARY

Government is the institution through which a society makes and enforces its **public policies**—all those things a government decides to do. Every government has three kinds of power: **legislative power,** or the power to establish law; **executive power,** or the power to carry out the law; and **judicial power,** or the power to interpret laws and settle disputes. These powers are often outlined in a **constitution**—the body of laws that sets out a government's structure, principles, and processes.

In a **dictatorship,** one person or a small group may exercise all the powers of government. In a **democracy,** supreme authority over government rests with the people.

The world's dominant political unit is the **state**—a body of people living in a defined territory, often called a nation or country. Every state has a **sovereign** government, or one with absolute power.

The Preamble to the U.S. Constitution describes the goals of the United States' Federal Government. It says that government should form a more perfect union, or keep the States working together; establish justice; ensure domestic tranquility, or keep order; provide for the common defense; promote the general welfare; and secure the blessings of liberty.

> ### THE **BIG** IDEA
>
> **A government enables a society to carry out its policies and protect its citizens from violence and injustice.**

■ GRAPHIC SUMMARY: *Structure of Government*

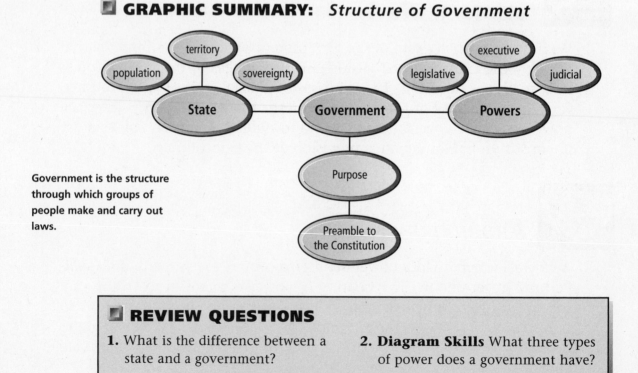

Government is the structure through which groups of people make and carry out laws.

■ REVIEW QUESTIONS

1. What is the difference between a state and a government?

2. Diagram Skills What three types of power does a government have?

FORMS OF GOVERNMENT

◪ TEXT SUMMARY

Governments may be classified in three ways. The first is defined by who may participate in the government. In a democracy, supreme political authority rests with the people. All dictatorships are authoritarian, meaning that the ruler holds absolute authority over the people. A dictatorship may be totalitarian, meaning that the rulers control nearly every aspect of human affairs. It may also be an **autocracy**—in which one person holds unlimited political power—or an **oligarchy**—in which a small elite holds the power to rule.

The second classification is defined by where government power is held. In a **unitary government,** a single, central agency holds all governmental powers. In a **federal government,** a central government and several local governments share governmental powers in a **division of powers.** Because the Constitution divides power between the National Government and the States, the United States is a federal government. A federal system is different from a **confederation,** which is an alliance of independent states.

The third type of classification describes the relationship between the legislative and the executive branches of government. A **presidential government** divides power between the branches, while a **parliamentary government** focuses power on the legislative branch. In the latter, the executive branch is chosen by and subject to the legislative branch.

THE **BIG** IDEA

The United States is a democracy with a federal and presidential system of government.

◪ GRAPHIC SUMMARY:
Classifications of Government

The government of the United States is a federal, presidential democracy.

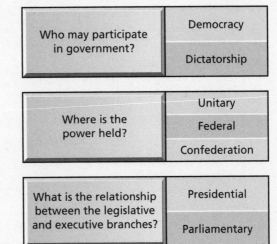

Who may participate in government?	Democracy
	Dictatorship

Where is the power held?	Unitary
	Federal
	Confederation

What is the relationship between the legislative and executive branches?	Presidential
	Parliamentary

◪ REVIEW QUESTIONS

1. How is the U.S. government an example of division of powers?

2. Chart Skills What are the three ways to classify governments?

BASIC CONCEPTS OF DEMOCRACY

▨ TEXT SUMMARY

The American concept of democracy rests on five basic notions. First, each individual has worth. Second, all individuals are equal. Third, the majority of the people rules, but the majority must respect the rights of any minority. Fourth, **compromise,** or the blending and adjusting of competing interests, is necessary. Fifth, each individual must have the widest possible degree of freedom.

The American commitment to freedom is evident in the nation's economic system. This system, often called the **free enterprise system,** is based on private ownership, individual initiative, profit, and competition. Also known as capitalism, this system does not rely on the government to make economic decisions. Rather, individuals make those decisions through the **law of supply and demand.** That law says that when supplies of goods and services become plentiful, prices tend to drop; when supplies become scarcer, prices tend to rise. The American economic system is most accurately called a **mixed economy** because the United States government does play a role in the economy by regulating and promoting it.

THE **BIG** IDEA

Democracy rests on the rights and freedoms of individuals; the American commitment to these ideals is evident in its free enterprise system.

▨ GRAPHIC SUMMARY: *The Basic Notions of American Democracy*

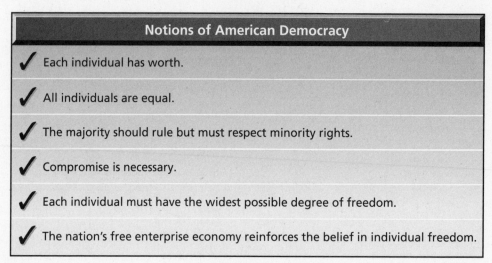

Notions of American Democracy
✓ Each individual has worth.
✓ All individuals are equal.
✓ The majority should rule but must respect minority rights.
✓ Compromise is necessary.
✓ Each individual must have the widest possible degree of freedom.
✓ The nation's free enterprise economy reinforces the belief in individual freedom.

The American government and economy are both rooted in a deep commitment to individual freedom.

▨ REVIEW QUESTIONS

1. How does the law of supply and demand work?

2. Chart Skills How does the United States' free enterprise economy relate to individual freedom?

CHAPTER 1 *Test*

◼ IDENTIFYING MAIN IDEAS

Write the letter of the correct answer in the blank provided. (10 points each)

____ 1. A constitution

   A. sets out the processes of a government.
   B. sets out the structure of a government.
   C. sets out the principles of a government.
   D. all of the above

____ 2. In which type of government does one person rule?

   A. a democracy
   B. a dictatorship
   C. a presidential government
   D. a unitary government

____ 3. By definition, a state must have a body of people with a defined territory and

   A. a sovereign government.
   B. an oligarchy.
   C. a democracy.
   D. a constitution.

____ 4. All dictatorships are

   A. totalitarian.
   B. representative.
   C. authoritarian.
   D. parliamentary.

____ 5. The government of the United States is

   A. federal.
   B. unitary.
   C. parliamentary.
   D. authoritarian.

____ 6. In a democracy, supreme authority belongs to the

   A. state.
   B. people.
   C. elite.
   D. rulers.

____ 7. A unitary system of government is characterized by

   A. a single center of power.
   B. rulers who control every aspect of human affairs.
   C. a division of power between a central government and local governments.
   D. one dominant branch of government.

____ 8. Which of the following must accompany majority rule in the American concept of democracy?

   A. absolute freedom
   B. totalitarian rule
   C. presidential government
   D. respect for minority rights

____ 9. In a presidential government,

   A. the president and legislature are always of the same political party.
   B. the president is chosen by the legislature.
   C. the executive and legislative branches share powers.
   D. the executive and legislative branches have the same powers.

____ 10. The economy of the United States is best described as

   A. capitalism.
   B. a mixed economy.
   C. a free economy.
   D. supply and demand.

Origins of American Government

SECTION 1 OUR POLITICAL BEGINNINGS

▨ TEXT SUMMARY

The colonists brought with them to North America knowledge of the English political system, including three key ideas about government. The first idea was that of ordered government. This means that a government's rules should help people get along. The second idea, of **limited government**, means that government has restricted powers. The third idea, of **representative government**, means that government should serve the people.

The English tradition of government grew from three landmark documents. The **Magna Carta** (1215) said that the king did not have total power, and it protected the rights of trial by jury and due process of law. The **Petition of Right** (1628) said the king could not use the military to rule during peacetime or let soldiers live in people's homes. The **English Bill of Rights** (1689) forbade keeping an army during peacetime, guaranteed a fair and speedy trial, and ensured that all parliamentary elections were free.

The three types of English colonies each provided training for the colonists in the art of government. Each colony was based on a **charter,** a written grant of authority from the king. Royal colonies were ruled directly by the Crown. **Proprietary** colonies were organized by an owner to whom the king had granted land. Charter colonies were based on charters granted directly to the colonists. Most colonies had **bicameral** (two-house) legislatures, although Pennsylvania's was **unicameral** (one-house).

> ### THE **BIG** IDEA
>
> The English tradition of ordered, limited, and representative government served as the basis of colonial governments.

▨ GRAPHIC SUMMARY: *Landmark English Documents*

Bill of Rights 1689 • Prohibited keeping an army in peacetime. Required free parliamentary elections. Guaranteed right to a fair trial. Forbade cruel and unusual punishments and excessive bail.

Petition of Right 1628 • King could not imprison subjects without the lawful judgment of their peers or by rule of law. King could not impose military rule in peacetime. King could not force unwilling citizens to house soldiers.

Magna Carta 1215 • Limited the power of the king. Protected right to trial by jury and due process of law.

From these three English documents colonists took the basic ideas used to form their own governments.

▨ REVIEW QUESTIONS

1. What were the three key ideas about government in the English tradition?

2. **Diagram Skills** What document first protected the right to a trial by jury?

SECTION 2 — THE COMING OF INDEPENDENCE

■ TEXT SUMMARY

Great Britain became more involved in ruling its colonies in the 1760s. It created new taxes and laws that caused the colonists to object to "taxation without representation."

The colonists reacted to the changes in British policy by taking small steps toward unity. The New England States had already formed a **confederation,** or union for a common purpose, in the 1600s. In 1754, Benjamin Franklin's **Albany Plan of Union** proposed a congress of **delegates** from all colonies, but both the colonies and the king rejected it.

Twelve of the thirteen colonies joined at the First Continental Congress in 1774. They met to plan opposition to harsh British policies and punishment of colonists who resisted. One form of opposition was to **boycott,** or refuse to buy,

British goods. The colonists hoped to force the British to **repeal,** or recall, their hated policies.

Finally, the colonists were ready to fight. The American Revolution began on April 19, 1775. On May 10, 1775, the Second Continental Congress began. It became the first government of the new United States and produced the Declaration of Independence.

The newly formed States wrote constitutions. A constitution is the basic set of laws that creates a government. The State constitutions all shared the principle of **popular sovereignty,** meaning that government can exist only with the consent of the people governed.

> THE **BIG** IDEA
>
> As British policies led them toward independence, the colonies developed new forms of government.

■ GRAPHIC SUMMARY: *Creating the United States, 1770–1790*

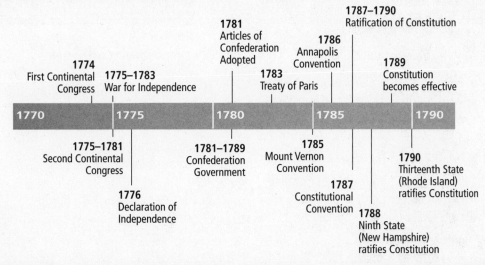

With the start of the American Revolution in 1775, the colonies needed to replace their British governments.

■ REVIEW QUESTIONS

1. What was the first government of the United States called?

2. **Time Line Skills** For how long did the Second Continental Congress meet?

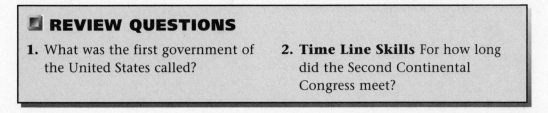

 **SECTION 3** # THE CRITICAL PERIOD

◼ TEXT SUMMARY

The 1780s were problem-filled years for the United States. Although the States wanted a permanent government, they did not want to give it much power.

The 13 States **ratified**—or formally approved—the **Articles of Confederation** in 1781. The Articles set up a government that tied the States together in a loose union. They also created a central government that had power to do little more than set up an army and a navy, make war and peace, and settle State disputes. This government consisted of only one branch, the Congress, which was unicameral. Each State had one vote. Each year, Congress was to choose one of its members as its **presiding officer,** or chairperson.

The National Government had no power to make the States obey the Articles or the laws passed by the legislature. The States had the power to tax and printed their own money. When a rebellion broke out in Massachusetts, many leaders were convinced that Americans had to strengthen the government.

Delegates from Maryland and Virginia met at Mount Vernon, Virginia, to solve their trade problems. Their success led them to call a meeting at Annapolis, Maryland, to try to solve some of the nation's problems. Only five States sent delegates. They set up another meeting in Philadelphia, Pennsylvania which became the Constitutional Convention.

> **THE BIG IDEA**
>
> The weaknesses of the Articles of Confederation led to demands for a stronger central government.

◼ GRAPHIC SUMMARY: *Weaknesses of the Government under the Articles of Confederation*

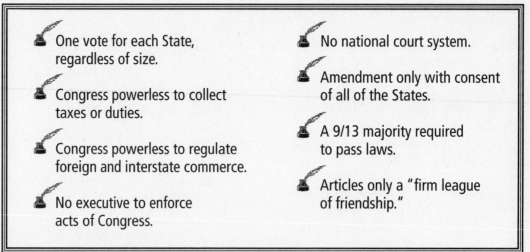

- One vote for each State, regardless of size.
- Congress powerless to collect taxes or duties.
- Congress powerless to regulate foreign and interstate commerce.
- No executive to enforce acts of Congress.
- No national court system.
- Amendment only with consent of all of the States.
- A 9/13 majority required to pass laws.
- Articles only a "firm league of friendship."

Under the Articles of Confederation, the new central government had few powers.

◼ REVIEW QUESTIONS

1. What were the Articles of Confederation?

2. **Chart Skills** List three weaknesses of the government under the Articles of Confederation.

SECTION 4 CREATING THE CONSTITUTION

◼ TEXT SUMMARY

In 1787, 55 delegates from 12 States met in Philadelphia to revise the Articles of Confederation. Later known as the **Framers,** these delegates soon decided to write a new constitution instead.

The delegates from Virginia were the first to offer a plan. The **Virginia Plan** called for three branches of government: an executive, a bicameral legislature, and courts. The number of representatives a State sent to the legislature was linked to its wealth and population. Small States opposed this plan.

The **New Jersey Plan** called for a government without strong and separate branches. It also proposed a unicameral legislature with an equal number of representatives from each State.

The **Connecticut Compromise** combined the basic features of the Virginia and New Jersey plans. It called for two houses in Congress. In the smaller Senate, the States would have equal representation. In the larger House, each State would be represented based on its population.

The Constitution became a document of compromises. The **Three-Fifths Compromise** determined that States could count three-fifths of their slaves as part of their populations, which increased their representation in the House. The **Commerce and Slave Trade Compromise** forbade Congress from taxing exports from any State as well as from acting against the slave trade for 20 years. The Framers made many other compromises before they completed their work on September 17, 1787.

THE BIG IDEA

The delegates to the Constitutional Convention created a new form of government for a new nation.

◼ GRAPHIC SUMMARY: *Compromises Made in Framing the Constitution*

Compromise	Issue	Solution
Connecticut	Representation in Congress	Bicameral legislature: States have equal representation in Senate; representation in the House depends on State's population.
Three-Fifths	Counting slaves within population to determine representation	Slaves were counted as if 3/5 of one person, both for representation and taxation.
Commerce and Slave Trade	Granting Congress the power to regulate foreign and interstate trade	Congress was forbidden to tax a State's exports or take action against the slave trade for 20 years.

The Framers made many compromises when writing the Constitution.

◼ REVIEW QUESTIONS

1. Why did small States oppose the Virginia Plan?

2. **Chart Skills** Which compromise guaranteed that the slave trade could exist for 20 years?

RATIFYING THE CONSTITUTION

▉ TEXT SUMMARY

The Framers had provided that before the Constitution could take effect, at least nine of the 13 States had to ratify it. Americans were greatly divided in their opinions about the Constitution.

Two groups formed during the ratification process: the **Federalists,** who favored ratifying the Constitution, and the **Anti-Federalists,** who strongly opposed it.

The Federalists stressed the weaknesses of the Articles of Confederation. Anti-Federalists attacked almost every part of the Constitution, but two of its features drew the strongest criticism: (1) the greatly increased powers of the central government and (2) the lack of a bill of rights that would provide for basic liberties such as freedom of speech and religion.

The struggle for ratification was intense in several States, especially Virginia and New York. The Federalists finally won in both States.

After eleven States had ratified the Constitution in 1788, the States held elections for a new President. The first Congress of the new National Government met in March, 1789. Because there was not a **quorum,** or majority of its members, the electoral votes could not be counted until April 6. At that point, it declared George Washington President.

> ### THE **BIG** IDEA
>
> After great debate, the Constitution was ratified by nine States and became the supreme law of the nation.

▉ GRAPHIC SUMMARY: *The Debate over Ratification*

Federalists
- Favored Constitution.
- Believed Constitution was strong enough to solve country's problems.
- Led by Alexander Hamilton and James Madison.

Anti-Federalists
- Opposed Constitution.
- Believed Constitution was too strong. Wanted a bill of rights added to protect individual freedoms.
- Led by Patrick Henry and John Hancock.

The debate over ratification of the Constitution was intense.

▉ REVIEW QUESTIONS

1. Who were the Federalists?

2. **Diagram Skills** Give two reasons why the Anti-Federalists opposed the Constitution.

CHAPTER 2 *Test*

■ IDENTIFYING MAIN IDEAS

Write the letter of the correct answer in the blank provided. (10 points each)

____ 1. A representative government

  A. serves the people.
  B. creates rules to help the people get along.
  C. has restricted powers.
  D. is ruled by a king.

____ 2. What is the Magna Carta?

  A. a plan for a new government of the United States
  B. a colonial American document listing people's rights under the Constitution
  C. an English document that limited the powers of the king
  D. an attempt by Benjamin Franklin to unite the colonies

____ 3. The first National Government for the Unites States was

  A. the First Continental Congress.
  B. the Second Continental Congress.
  C. the Articles of Confederation.
  D. the Constitution of the Unites States.

____ 4. Which of the following was a plan of government for the States during the war of independence?

  A. the Albany Plan of Union
  B. the Articles of Confederation
  C. the Declaration of Independence
  D. the Petition of Right

____ 5. Each of the State constitutions written during the Revolution provided for

  A. a bill of rights.
  B. a governor.
  C. a unicameral legislature.
  D. the principle of popular sovereignty.

____ 6. The government formed by the Articles of Confederation is best described as

  A. a strong national government.
  B. a government controlled by the king and Parliament.

  C. a union of States led by a President with almost unlimited power.
  D. a firm league of friendship.

____ 7. The Virginia Plan called for

  A. counting slaves as three-fifths of a person.
  B. a government with three separate branches.
  C. a legislature with one house.
  D. a bill of rights.

____ 8. The Connecticut Compromise called for a legislature

  A. made up of two houses. In one house, the representatives would be elected by the States; the President would appoint the members of the second house.
  B. made up of one house in which each State had one vote.
  C. made up of two houses. In the smaller house all States would be represented equally; in the larger house, representation would be decided by population.
  D. made up of one house in which States were represented according to their wealth and population.

____ 9. Before the Constitution could become law, how many States had to ratify it?

  A. 1
  B. 9
  C. 11
  D. 13

____ 10. Who won the debate over ratifying the Constitution?

  A. the colonists
  B. the Federalists
  C. the representatives
  D. the Anti-Federalists

CHAPTER 3

The Constitution

SECTION 1   *THE SIX BASIC PRINCIPLES*

■ TEXT SUMMARY

The Constitution originally consisted of a **Preamble,** or introduction, and seven sections called **articles.** The Framers developed the Preamble and articles around the six broad ideas, or principles, described below.

Popular sovereignty is the idea that the people are the source of all power held by the government.

Limited government means that the government possesses only the powers the people give it—it must obey the Constitution. This principle is also known as **constitutionalism.** Government officials are subject to the **rule of law**—they must always obey the law and are never above it.

Separation of powers establishes three separate parts, or branches, that share the government's power. These branches are the executive, the legislative, and the judicial.

The Constitution uses a system of **checks and balances** to ensure that none of the three branches can become too powerful. Each branch has ways to limit the power of the other two. An example of this principle is the power of the President to **veto,** or reject, any act of Congress. Congress may then override a veto with a two-thirds vote in each house.

Judicial review is the power of the courts to decide what the Constitution means. The courts also have the power to declare a government action to be against the Constitution, or **unconstitutional.**

Lastly, the Framers used the principle of **federalism** to divide power between the central government and the States.

> ### THE **BIG** IDEA
>
> The Constitution is based on six broad principles: popular sovereignty, limited government, separation of powers, checks and balances, judicial review, and federalism.

■ GRAPHIC SUMMARY: *Six Constitutional Principles*

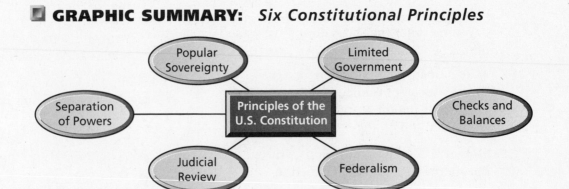

The Constitution and the government of the United States are based on these six ideas.

■ REVIEW QUESTIONS

1. Explain the principle of federalism.

2. **Diagram Skills** Which principle divides the government into three branches?

FORMAL AMENDMENT

TEXT SUMMARY

The Constitution has lasted more than 200 years because it has changed with the times. Many of its words and their meanings are the same, but some words have been changed, eliminated, or added—and some of the meanings have been modified as well. The alterations to the Constitution have occurred in two ways: either through formal or informal **amendments,** or changes.

A **formal amendment** is a change to the Constitution's written words. The Framers created four ways to make such changes. (See the Graphic Summary.) The Framers followed the principle of federalism in creating these methods. First, amendments are proposed, or suggested, at a national level—either by Congress or at a national convention. Then they are ratified at the State level—either in the State legislatures or by State conventions. Method 1 has been used for all but one of the 27 amendments.

The first ten amendments are the **Bill of Rights.** Congress proposed all of them in 1789 because many people refused to support the Constitution unless the Federal Government protected these basic rights. The States approved these ten amendments in 1791. The other 17 amendments became part of the Constitution one at a time.

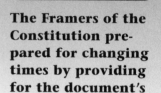

THE **BIG** IDEA

The Framers of the Constitution prepared for changing times by providing for the document's formal amendment.

GRAPHIC SUMMARY: *Methods of Formal Amendment*

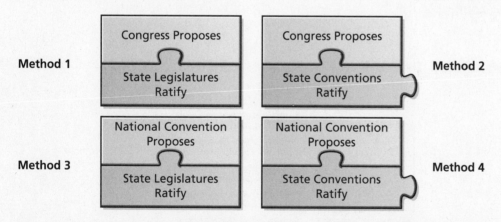

Method 1
Congress Proposes
State Legislatures Ratify

Method 2
Congress Proposes
State Conventions Ratify

Method 3
National Convention Proposes
State Legislatures Ratify

Method 4
National Convention Proposes
State Conventions Ratify

Each of the methods of formally amending the Constitution is based on the principle of federalism.

REVIEW QUESTIONS

1. What is a formal amendment to the Constitution?

2. Diagram Skills Which two bodies may ratify formal amendments to the Constitution?

CONSTITUTIONAL CHANGE BY OTHER MEANS

◪ TEXT SUMMARY

Many informal changes to the Constitution have been made since 1787. Unlike formal amendments, these changes have not altered the Constitution's actual words. These changes have come from five sources.

1. Congress has made changes to the Constitution through two kinds of basic legislation. First, it has passed laws that fill in details about the specific ways the government operates. Second, it has passed thousands of laws that explain certain parts of the Constitution.

2. The way Presidents have used their powers has produced some informal changes. For example, a President may choose to make an **executive agreement,** or pact, with the head of another country instead of a **treaty,** or a formal agreement between two sovereign countries that requires congressional approval.

3. The courts, especially the U.S. Supreme Court, have informally changed the Constitution by explaining parts of it when ruling on cases. They also decide if government actions are constitutional.

4. Political parties have informally shaped what the government does. For example, the parties have decreased the importance of the **electoral college,** the group that formally selects the nation's President.

5. Customs are the usual ways people do things. Many customs have developed in American government that are not mentioned in the Constitution. For example, the President's **Cabinet,** or advisory body, is customarily made up of the heads of executive departments and other officers. **Senatorial courtesy** is a custom in which the Senate will not approve a presidential appointment to serve in a State if the appointment is opposed by a senator from the President's party.

> ### THE **BIG** IDEA
>
> **Many changes to the Constitution have been made by informal means.**

◪ GRAPHIC SUMMARY: *Sources of Constitutional Change*

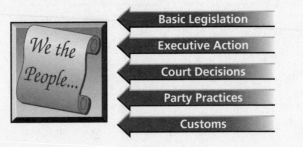

Basic Legislation

Executive Action

Court Decisions

Party Practices

Customs

The Constitution has been changed many times by informal means.

◪ REVIEW QUESTIONS

1. How does the Constitution change by other than formal amendment?

2. Diagram Skills Name two governmental bodies that may make informal changes.

CHAPTER 3 *Test*

◼ IDENTIFYING MAIN IDEAS

Write the letter of the correct answer in the blank provided. (10 points each)

____ 1. Popular sovereignty means that

    A. the States have more power than the Federal Government.

    B. the courts may decide what the words of the Constitution mean.

    C. the Constitution may be amended, or changed.

    D. all government power belongs to the people.

____ 2. Which of the following is an example of checks and balances?

    A. The U.S. Supreme Court declares that a law is unconstitutional.

    B. Power is divided between the Federal Government and the States.

    C. The Senate observes senatorial courtesy.

    D. Congress passes a law.

____ 3. The principle of government that favors a national government with three independent branches is called

    A. separation of powers.

    B. federalism.

    C. formal amendment.

    D. executive action.

____ 4. The first ten amendments to the Constitution are called the

    A. treaties.

    B. vetoes.

    C. Bill of Rights.

    D. executive actions.

____ 5. At the present time, the number of formal amendments to the Constitution is

    A. 10.

    B. 15.

    C. 27.

    D. 100.

____ 6. The methods of formally amending the Constitution follow the principle of

    A. limited government.

    B. federalism.

    C. separation of powers.

    D. judicial review.

____ 7. Which method of amending the Constitution has been used for all but one of its formal amendments?

    A. Congress proposes/State conventions ratify

    B. National convention proposes/State legislatures ratify

    C. National convention proposes/State conventions ratify

    D. Congress proposes/State legislatures ratify

____ 8. Congress can informally change the Constitution by

    A. passing laws.

    B. proposing amendments.

    C. declaring laws unconstitutional.

    D. taking executive action.

____ 9. Which is an example of informal constitutional change by executive action?

    A. A political party holds a convention to choose its candidate for President.

    B. Congress passes a law about the operation of the United States Postal Service.

    C. The President makes an executive agreement with another country instead of a formal treaty.

    D. The President issues an executive order.

____ 10. The presidential appointment of Supreme Court justices is an example of

    A. formal amendment.

    B. checks and balances.

    C. vetoes.

    D. judicial review.

Federalism

SECTION 1 FEDERALISM: THE DIVISION OF POWER

■ TEXT SUMMARY

Federalism is the system of government in which a written constitution divides the powers of government. The U.S. Constitution provides for the **division of powers** between two levels—the National Government and the States.

The National Government possesses **delegated powers**—powers specifically given by the Constitution. Most of these are **exclusive powers,** or powers that belong only to the National Government.

There are three kinds of delegated powers. **Expressed powers** are those listed in the Constitution. **Implied powers** are not listed but are suggested. **Inherent powers** are those that national govern-ments have historically possessed, such as the regulation of immigration. Some pow-ers delegated to the National Government are **concurrent powers.** It shares these powers with the State governments.

The States' powers are called **reserved powers.** They are powers not already given to the National Government and not listed as powers the States may not have. For example, the States may decide how old people must be to get drivers' licenses.

Since some of the powers of the National and State governments overlap, the Supreme Court plays the key role of resolving disputes. As part of this job, it applies the Constitution's Supremacy Clause, which states that the Constitution is the "supreme Law of the Land."

> **THE BIG IDEA**
>
> Federalism divides the powers of the United States government between the National Government and the States.

■ GRAPHIC SUMMARY: *The Division of Powers*

National Powers	Concurrent Powers	State Powers
• Coin money • Regulate interstate and foreign trade • Raise and maintain armed forces • Declare war • Govern U.S. territories and admit new States • Conduct foreign relations	• Levy and collect taxes • Borrow money • Establish courts • Define crimes and set punishments • Claim private property for public use	• Regulate trade and business within the State • Establish public schools • Pass license requirements for professionals • Regulate alcoholic beverages • Conduct elections • Establish local governments

The federal system determines the way in which powers are divided and shared between the National and State governments.

■ REVIEW QUESTIONS

1. What is the difference between exclusive powers and concurrent powers?

2. Diagram Skills Which level of government establishes schools?

THE NATIONAL GOVERNMENT AND THE 50 STATES

◼ TEXT SUMMARY

The Constitution says that the National Government must guarantee a "Republican Form of Government" and protect the States "against Invasion" and against "domestic Violence." This last statement allows federal officials to enter a State to restore order or to help in a disaster.

The National Government may create new States but not from the territory of an existing State without permission from that State's legislature. To become a new State, an area's residents must first ask Congress for admission. Congress passes an **enabling act,** which approves the writing of a State constitution. The area's residents write the constitution and submit it to Congress. Congress makes the area a State with an **act of admission.** When the President signs the act, the State is admitted to the Union.

The National Government and States cooperate in many ways. From 1972 to 1987, Congress gave the States and their local governments a share of federal tax money through **revenue sharing.** Through the three types of **grants-in-aid program,** the National Government gives resources to the States or their local governments. **Categorical grants** are made for specified purposes. **Block grants** are given for much broader purposes. **Project grants** are made to States, localities, and even private agencies that apply for them.

In turn, States assist the National Government in many ways. For example, the State and local governments carry out and pay for national elections.

THE BIG IDEA

The Constitution allows and requires the National Government to help the States in certain ways.

◼ GRAPHIC SUMMARY: *National and State Cooperation*

National Government

• Guarantees a republican form of government
• Protects against invasions and domestic violence
• Admits new States
• Provides three types of grants-in-aid:
block grants; categorical grants; project grants

State Governments

• Conduct national elections
• Admit new citizens in State courts
• Cooperate with federal law enforcement agencies

The National Government and the States cooperate in many ways.

◼ REVIEW QUESTIONS

1. How does an area become a State?

2. Diagram Skills What are two ways in which States may help the National Government?

SECTION 3 · INTERSTATE RELATIONS

◪ TEXT SUMMARY

Trouble among the States was a major reason for the adoption of the Constitution. As a result, several parts of the document deal with how the States interact. For example, the Constitution forbids States to make treaties with one another. However, they may make **interstate compacts,** or agreements in response to shared problems.

The **Full Faith and Credit Clause** of the Constitution says that each State must honor the laws, records, and court decisions of every other State. This clause applies only to civil matters, not criminal matters.

The Constitution's **Privileges and Immunities Clause** says that no State may discriminate against a person who

lives in another State. Thus each State must recognize the right of any American to travel in, do business in, or become a resident of that State. However, a State may draw reasonable distinctions between its own residents and those of other States. For example, a State may require that a person live within its boundaries for a period of time before voting.

The Constitution also establishes **extradition,** the legal process by which a person accused of a crime in one State is returned for trial to that State by the police of another State.

The Constitution's provisions about interstate relations strengthened the hand of the National Government. By doing so, they lessened many of the frictions between the States.

> ### THE **BIG** IDEA
>
> **Several provisions of the Constitution deal with the States' relations with one another.**

◪ GRAPHIC SUMMARY: *Interstate Relations*

Interstate Compacts	States may make agreements about solving shared problems
Full Faith and Credit	Each State must honor the laws, records, and court decisions of every other State.
Privileges and Immunities	No State may discriminate against a person who lives in another State.
Extradition	Legal process by which a fugitive from justice in one State is returned to it from another State.

Several key provisions of the Constitution promote cooperation between and among the States.

◪ REVIEW QUESTIONS

1. What is the reason for extradition?

2. Chart Skills What is the purpose of interstate compacts?

Name _____ Class _____ Date _____

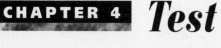

◼ IDENTIFYING MAIN IDEAS

Write the letter of the correct answer in the blank provided. (10 points each)

____ 1. What is the constitutional division of powers?

  A. the creation of the three branches of government
  B. the delegation of specific powers to the National Government
  C. the powers given to the National Government simply because it is the National Government
  D. the assigning of certain powers to the National Government and certain ones to the States

____ 2. Powers shared by both the National Government and the States are called

  A. concurrent powers.
  B. inherent powers.
  C. expressed powers.
  D. reserved powers.

____ 3. The reserved powers belong to the

  A. National Government.
  B. States.
  C. Congress.
  D. President.

____ 4. The process of admitting a new State begins with

  A. an invitation from Congress.
  B. congressional review of the potential State's constitution.
  C. the area's residents asking Congress for admission.
  D. a vote in neighboring States.

____ 5. A new State may not be created

  A. without the permission of all existing State legislatures.
  B. without a constitutional amendment.
  C. without a favorable decision of the Supreme Court.
  D. from the territory of an existing State without its permission.

____ 6. In the 1800s, the National Government gave many States land to sell to fund State universities. This action is an example of

  A. an enabling act.
  B. a grant-in-aid program.
  C. an act of admission.
  D. revenue sharing.

____ 7. Which kind of grant-in-aid has to be applied for?

  A. a categorical grant
  B. a project grant
  C. revenue sharing
  D. a block grant

____ 8. What part of the Constitution stops each State from discriminating against residents of other States?

  A. the Privileges and Immunities Clause
  B. the Full Faith and Credit Clause
  C. the First Amendment
  D. the Preamble

____ 9. States must honor each other's laws and court decisions according to the

  A. Fifth Amendment.
  B. Full Faith and Credit Clause.
  C. Privileges and Immunities Clause.
  D. act of admission.

____ 10. A person robs a bank in Mississippi and drives to Tennessee. The legal process by which Tennessee police will return the person to Mississippi to stand trial is called

  A. grants-in-aid.
  B. checks and balances.
  C. federalism.
  D. extradition.

CHAPTER 5

Political Parties

SECTION 1 *PARTIES AND WHAT THEY DO*

◼ TEXT SUMMARY

A **political party** is a group of people who try to control government by winning elections and holding public offices. The United States' two **major parties** are the Republicans and the Democrats.

Political parties are essential to democratic government. Parties help link the people and their wishes to government action. Parties also help unify the people by finding compromise among contending views.

Political parties perform five major functions. First, they nominate, or name, candidates for public office. Parties present these candidates to the voters and then gather support for them.

Second, parties inform the people and inspire them to participate in public affairs. Third, political parties help ensure that their candidates and officeholders are qualified and of good character.

Fourth, political parties have some governing responsibilities. Congress and State legislatures are organized along party lines. They conduct much of their business based on **partisanship,** or firm allegiance to a political party. Fifth, parties act as watchdogs over the conduct of government. The party out of power keeps an especially close eye on the policies and behavior of the **party in power,** or the party that controls the executive branch of each national or State government.

> **THE BIG IDEA**
>
> Political parties, essential to democratic government, shape the way government works and perform important functions.

◼ GRAPHIC SUMMARY: *Functions of Political Parties*

Function	Explanation
Nominate candidates	Select and gain support for candidates for office
Inform and inspire voters	Inform people about and stimulate interest in public affairs
Ensure candidate quality	Try to ensure that candidates and officeholders are qualified and of good character
Help govern	Operate on partisan lines in Congress and State legislatures
Act as watchdogs	Observe and criticize the operation of government, especially officials of the other party

Political parties perform five important functions in American government.

◼ REVIEW QUESTIONS

1. What is a political party?

2. Chart Skills How does a political party act as a watchdog?

THE TWO-PARTY SYSTEM

◼ TEXT SUMMARY

In the United States, there is a **two-party system,** which means that two major political parties dominate politics. **Minor parties,** or those without wide support, also exist.

The first two American political parties arose during the ratification of the Constitution; several factors have made the two-party system last. One basic factor is tradition; the system remains because it has always been.

Also, the electoral system favors a two-party system. Nearly all U.S. elections are **single-member district** elections, in which voters choose only one candidate for each office. The winner is whoever receives a **plurality,** or the largest number of votes. Most voters tend not to vote for minor party candidates, who are unlikely to win. Also, much of U.S. election law—created by Republicans and Democrats together, or in a **bipartisan** way—discourages minor parties.

The United States is a **pluralistic society,** or one that consists of distinct cultures and groups. Still, there exists a broad **consensus**—a general agreement among various groups—on fundamental matters. Consensus helps eliminate the need for many parties.

However, alternative political systems exist around the world. In a **multiparty** arrangement, several major and minor parties compete. To gain power, a number of parties often form a **coalition,** or a union of people with diverse interests who will share power. Nearly all dictatorships today have **one-party systems,** in which only one party is allowed.

THE **BIG** IDEA

The United States' two-party system is a result of history; several factors have helped maintain it over time.

◼ GRAPHIC SUMMARY: *Factors Behind a Two-Party System*

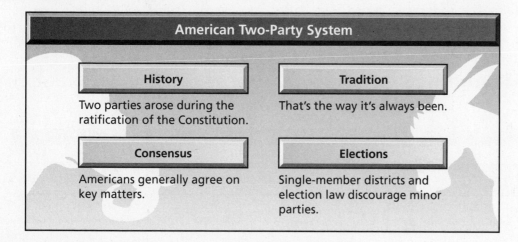

American Two-Party System

History	**Tradition**
Two parties arose during the ratification of the Constitution.	That's the way it's always been.
Consensus	**Elections**
Americans generally agree on key matters.	Single-member districts and election law discourage minor parties.

Four main factors account for the two-party system in the United States.

◼ REVIEW QUESTIONS

1. Why do minor party candidates have little chance of winning in American elections?

2. Chart Skills What four factors account for the two-party system in the United States?

THE TWO-PARTY SYSTEM IN AMERICAN HISTORY

◼ TEXT SUMMARY

Debate over the Constitution's ratification caused two sides—the Federalists and the Anti-Federalists—to form. These became the first political parties.

In the election of 1800, Anti-Federalist Thomas Jefferson beat the **incumbent,** that is, the current officeholder, Federalist President John Adams. The Anti-Federalists then took control of politics. They later became the Democratic-Republicans and then the Democrats.

There have been four eras during which one party dominated national politics. From 1800 to 1860, the Democrats held power. They were a coalition of small farmers, debtors, frontier pioneers, and slaveholders. By the mid-1820s, they had split into **factions,** or dissenting groups.

In 1854 the Republican Party formed. It controlled national politics from 1860 to 1932. The party was supported by business and financial interests, farmers, laborers, and newly freed African Americans. By 1896 the Republicans drew from a broad range of the **electorate**—the people eligible to vote. At that time the nation's party politics began to move toward the economic arena and away from the **sectionalism,** or devotion to the interests of one region, that had plagued the nation for years.

The Great Depression had a huge impact on American life, and one change it saw was the return to dominance of the Democrats. From 1932 to 1968, they operated from a strong base of southerners, small farmers, labor union members, and city people.

A new era began in 1968 with the election of Republican President Richard Nixon. Since then, neither party has entirely dominated politics. For much of that time, while one party has held the White House, the other has controlled Congress.

THE **BIG** IDEA

The United States' two major political parties have a history of alternating control over government.

◼ GRAPHIC SUMMARY: *Political Parties in American History*

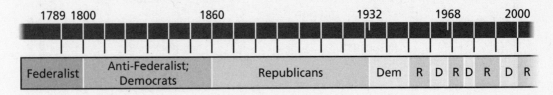

| 1789 1800 | | 1860 | | 1932 | | 1968 | | 2000 |

| Federalist | Anti-Federalist; Democrats | Republicans | Dem | R | D | R | D | R | D | R |

Control over national politics has gone back and forth between the parties since their beginning.

◼ REVIEW QUESTIONS

1. What were the first two American political parties called?

2. **Time Line Skills** When did the Republicans first begin to dominate national politics?

SECTION 4

THE MINOR PARTIES

TEXT SUMMARY

Four types of minor parties have played a role in American politics. **Ideological parties** are based on certain social, economic, or political ideas. They do not often win elections, but they remain active for a long time.

Single-issue parties focus on one public policy matter. They fade away after the issue has been resolved or people lose interest. Sometimes they are able to get one of the major parties to take on their issue.

Economic protest parties appear during tough financial times. They criticize the economic actions and plans of the major parties.

Most of the important minor parties in American politics have been **splinter parties**—parties that have broken away from one of the major parties. Usually they have a strong leader who did not win a major party's nomination.

Although most Americans do not support them, minor parties still have an impact on politics and on the major parties. The minor parties' members act as critics and innovators, drawing attention to otherwise neglected or controversial issues.

Strong third-party candidates can also play the "spoiler" role in elections. This means that they pull votes away from one of the major parties, weakening that party's ability to win an election.

> ### THE BIG IDEA
>
> Many minor parties have been active in American politics, and at times they have had important effects on elections and issues.

GRAPHIC SUMMARY: *The Four Types of Minor Parties*

Ideological Parties	Single-Issue Parties
Based on certain social, economic, or political ideas	Focus on one public policy matter
Not powerful but long-lasting	Fade away once issue has been resolved
Economic Protest Parties	**Splinter Parties**
Appear during tough financial times	Break away from a major party
Criticize the economic actions and plans of the major parties	Usually have a strong leader who lost a major party's nomination

The four types of minor parties form for different reasons.

REVIEW QUESTIONS

1. In what ways may minor parties affect politics?

2. Chart Skills Which type of minor party is formed by breaking away from a major party?

PARTY ORGANIZATION

▣ TEXT SUMMARY

The major parties are decentralized, or fragmented. At the national level, the party machinery has four basic elements: the national convention that nominates the party's candidates, the national committee that runs the party's affairs between conventions, the national chairperson who heads the national committee, and the congressional campaign committees that work to elect party members to Congress.

From the perspective of its members, a party has three basic and loosely connected parts. The party organization consists of the party machinery's leaders. The party in the electorate refers to those followers who usually vote for the party's candidates. The party in government describes the party's officeholders.

At the State and local levels, party structure is largely set by State law. At the State level, a central committee is headed by a chairperson. Local party structure varies widely, with a party unit for each district in which elections are held. The districts include congressional and legislative districts, counties, cities and towns, wards, and precincts. A **ward** is a small unit of a city; a **precinct** is a subdivision of a ward.

Political parties have been in decline since the 1960s. More and more voters regard themselves as independents. Also, **split-ticket voting,** or voting for candidates of different parties in the same election, has increased.

> ## THE **BIG** IDEA
>
> The structure of the major parties is decentralized; their different parts work together mostly during national elections.

▣ GRAPHIC SUMMARY: *Party Organization*

Party Organization	
National Party Machinery	**Basic Components of the Party**
national convention	party organization
national committee	party in the electorate
national chairperson	party in government
congressional campaign committees	

Political parties are fragmented, but work together.

▣ REVIEW QUESTIONS

1. What defines party structure at the State and local levels?

2. Chart Skills What are the major parts of the national party machinery?

CHAPTER 5 *Test*

■ IDENTIFYING MAIN IDEAS

Write the letter of the correct answer in the blank provided. (10 points each)

____ 1. What is a political party?

   A. a coalition of political leaders from every State
   B. an election in which the voters choose only one winner
   C. a group that tries to control government by winning elections and holding public office
   D. the voters

____ 2. Which is a function of a political party?

   A. to find candidates and gather support for them
   B. to nominate candidates for office
   C. to ensure that candidates are qualified
   D. all of the above

____ 3. The United States has a

   A. two-party system.
   B. multi-party system.
   C. one-party system.
   D. all of the above

____ 4. Factors contributing to the failure of minor parties to win much support in the United States include

   A. the electoral system.
   B. the number of independent voters.
   C. the loose structure of political parties.
   D. the pluralistic society of the United States.

____ 5. From 1932 to 1968, national politics was dominated by which party?

   A. the Republican Party
   B. a coalition of minor parties
   C. the Federalist Party
   D. the Democratic Party

____ 6. Since 1968 the government has been dominated by

   A. the Democrats.
   B. neither major party.
   C. the Republicans.
   D. minor parties.

____ 7. A minor party focused on solving one problem in American life is

   A. an ideological party.
   B. a splinter party.
   C. a single-issue party.
   D. an economic protest party.

____ 8. Minor parties play the "spoiler" role in elections by

   A. raising controversial issues.
   B. taking votes away from one of the major parties.
   C. using negative campaign advertisements.
   D. taking media attention away from the major parties.

____ 9. Which provides evidence that political parties are not as strong as they once were?

   A. the increasing number of independents
   B. the lack of straight-ticket voting
   C. increased spending on campaigns
   D. increased numbers of registered Democrats

____ 10. Members view party structure as including the party's leaders, the people who usually vote for the party, and

   A. independents.
   B. the party's officeholders.
   C. the national convention.
   D. the national chairperson.

Voters and Voter Behavior

SECTION 1 *THE RIGHT TO VOTE*

◾ TEXT SUMMARY

Suffrage, also called **franchise,** is the right to vote. In 1789 only white male property owners had this right. Today, the American **electorate,** or the people eligible to vote, includes nearly all citizens who are at least 18 years of age. Two trends caused this change: the elimination of many of the restrictions on suffrage and the assumption of much of the States' power over suffrage by the Federal Government.

The Constitution's Framers left the power to set suffrage qualifications to the States; they did, however, forbid States from setting different qualifications for who can vote in State and federal elections. Also, State qualifications could not violate any part of the Constitution.

The struggle to extend voting rights began in the early 1800s. Laws were passed to prevent States from restricting suffrage to the extent that they had been. By the mid-1800s, restrictions based on religion and property were eliminated, and nearly all white adult males could vote. In 1870 the 15th Amendment eliminated restrictions based on race; in practice, however, African Americans were not totally free to vote until the passage of several civil rights acts in the 1960s. In 1920 the 19th Amendment added women to the electorate. In 1964 the 24th Amendment said that States could not make the payment of a tax a condition for voting. Most recently, in 1971 the 26th Amendment said that States could not deny anyone 18 or older the right to vote.

> ## THE **BIG** IDEA
>
> **The United States has expanded its electorate through the elimination of restrictions on voting qualifications.**

◾ GRAPHIC SUMMARY: *The Expansion of Voting Rights*

Constitution	States cannot violate any part of the Constitution when they set suffrage requirements. States cannot have different qualifications for voting in State and federal elections.
15th Amendment (1870)	States cannot use race to determine who can vote.
19th Amendment (1920)	States cannot require people to be male to vote.
24th Amendment (1964)	States cannot use the payment of taxes to determine who can vote.
26th Amendment (1971)	States cannot require people to be older than 18 to vote.

Over time, the Constitution has been amended to allow for much less restriction on suffrage.

◾ REVIEW QUESTIONS

1. Who is eligible to vote in the United States today?

2. Chart Skills When did women win the right to vote?

VOTER QUALIFICATIONS

◪ TEXT SUMMARY

States decide voter qualifications. Over time, the qualifications have changed to include many more people.

Today, all States require voters to be citizens and legal residents of the State in which they wish to vote. In most cases, people must have lived in a State for a certain period of time before they may vote there—a practice meant to give people time to get to know the State's issues as well as to prevent outsiders from affecting local elections. Most States also forbid **transients,** or people living in a State for only a short time, from voting there.

There is also an age requirement for voting. In 1971 the 26th Amendment established 18 as the age at which a State may not deny a person the right to vote.

Forty-nine States—all except North Dakota—require voter **registration,** which is the act of signing up with local election officials. This requirement gives officials lists of registered voters, called **poll books.** State law tells officials to periodically review the poll books and purge them. **Purging** them means removing from them names of those no longer eligible to vote.

Today, no State has a voter requirement of **literacy**—the ability to read or write. Nor does any State require a **poll tax,** a tax paid for voting.

All States deny the right to vote to people in mental institutions or those legally considered mentally incompetent. Most States also deny the right to vote to anyone who has been convicted of a serious crime.

THE **BIG** IDEA

While all States have requirements for voting, most of those used to disenfranchise certain groups have been eliminated over time.

◪ GRAPHIC SUMMARY: *How States Decide Who Can Vote*

Voter Qualification	Status
State Citizenship	Required by all States
State Residence	Most States require 10–50 days, with an average of 30 days
Age	All States require a minimum age of 18
Voter Registration	Required by 49 States
Mental Competency	No State allows voting rights to anyone in a mental institution or legally considered mentally incompetent
Criminal Record	Most States deny voting rights to anyone convicted of a serious crime

Every State defines voter qualifications, although not all States require the same ones.

◪ REVIEW QUESTIONS

1. What is voter registration?

2. Chart Skills Name two groups of citizens who are denied the right to vote in most States.

SUFFRAGE AND CIVIL RIGHTS

◼ TEXT SUMMARY

In 1870 the 15th Amendment established that the right to vote may not be denied because of race. The amendment was ignored in some southern States, where tactics such as violence, threats, literacy testing, and gerrymandering were used to keep African Americans from voting. **Gerrymandering** is the drawing of electoral district lines in a way that limits a particular group's voting strength.

> ### THE **BIG** IDEA
>
> **Civil rights laws came about to protect Americans from being disenfranchised because of race.**

The civil rights movement pressured Congress to ensure African American voting rights. The Civil Rights Act of 1957 set up the Civil Rights Commission to investigate voter discrimination claims. The Civil Rights Act of 1960 called for federal referees to help all eligible people to register and vote in federal elections.

The Civil Rights Act of 1964 emphasized the use of **injunctions,** or orders from the courts to do or stop doing something, to ensure that eligible citizens were not kept from voting.

The Voting Rights Act of 1965 made the 15th Amendment truly effective by applying it to all elections—local, State, and federal. It forbade practices that prevented qualified voters from using the polls. Additionally, in those States where a majority of the electorate did not vote in 1964, this act gave the Department of Justice **preclearance,** or the right to approve new election laws, to prevent these laws from weakening minority voting rights. The act was to stay in effect for five years, but it has been extended three times and is now scheduled to expire in 2007.

◼ GRAPHIC SUMMARY: *Implementing the 15th Amendment over Time*

Not until the Voting Rights Act of 1965 did the 15th Amendment become fully effective.

1957 Civil Rights Act sets up the Civil Rights Commission to investigate voter discrimination claims.

1964 Civil Rights Act emphasizes the use of injunctions to prevent voter discrimination.

| 1870 | 1880 | 1890 | 1900 | 1910 | 1920 | 1930 | 1940 | 1950 | 1960 | 1970 |

Fifteenth Amendment establishes that the right to vote may not be denied because of race.

Civil Rights Act appoints federal voting referees to prevent voter discrimination.

1965 Voting Rights Act protects the rights of minority voters in all elections and forbids the use of practices that prevent qualified voters from using the polls.

◼ REVIEW QUESTIONS

1. How were injunctions used in the civil rights movement?

2. Time Line Skills When were minority voting rights ensured for *all* elections?

VOTER BEHAVIOR

◼ TEXT SUMMARY

Millions of Americans who are qualified to vote do not. Voter turnout is low for presidential elections and lower still for **off-year elections,** the congressional elections that are held between presidential elections.

Those who choose not to vote often lack a feeling of **political efficacy.** That means they do not feel that their votes make a difference. They are convinced that "government by the people" has been taken over by politicians, powerful special interests, and the media.

Studies of voter behavior focus on the results of particular elections, polls, and **political socialization**—the process by which people gain their political attitudes and opinions. These sources show that certain sociological factors—income, occupation, education, gender, age, religion, ethnicity, region of residence, and family—influence each person's voting choices. For example, there are measurable differences between the electoral choices of men and women, a phenomenon known as the **gender gap.**

Psychological factors—including party identification and perception of the candidates and issues—also contribute to voter behavior. **Party identification** is loyalty to a political party. A person loyal to one party may vote only for candidates of that party, a practice called **straight-ticket voting.** Many recent voters call themselves **independents,** or people not identified with a party. They may vote for candidates from both major parties in the same election, which is called **split-ticket voting.**

THE **BIG** IDEA

While low voter turnout is a serious problem, many factors influence the Americans who do vote.

◼ GRAPHIC SUMMARY: *Factors Influencing Voter Behavior*

Sociological Factors

Income	Religion
Occupation	Ethnicity
Education	Region of residence
Gender	Family
Age	

Voter Behavior

Psychological Factors

Party identification

Perception of candidates

Perception of issues

All kinds of factors influence the Americans who do vote.

◼ REVIEW QUESTIONS

1. How does political efficacy affect whether people choose to vote?

2. Diagram Skills Name five sociological factors that influence voter behavior.

CHAPTER 6 *Test*

▣ IDENTIFYING MAIN IDEAS

Write the letter of the correct answer in the blank provided. (10 points each)

____ 1. The Constitution forbids States to

   A. set the same requirements for voting in State and federal elections.
   B. set residence requirements for voters.
   C. set an age higher than 18 as the minimum age for voting.
   D. require voters to register.

____ 2. States may restrict a person's right to vote based on

   A. religion.
   B. mental competency.
   C. gender.
   D. tax payments.

____ 3. Which constitutional amendment forbids allowing only males to vote?

   A. 3rd
   B. 15th
   C. 19th
   D. 26th

____ 4. Most States forbid transients to vote because

   A. they do not pay taxes.
   B. they are not registered voters.
   C. they are not mentally competent.
   D. they will only be in the State for a short period of time.

____ 5. When a person registers to vote, he or she

   A. picks a political party to support.
   B. signs up with local election officials.
   C. purges poll books.
   D. chooses a candidate in an election.

____ 6. Some States tried to prevent African Americans from voting by using

   A. injunctions.
   B. political socialization.
   C. literacy tests.
   D. political efficacy.

____ 7. Which law made the 15th Amendment effective?

   A. the Voting Rights Act of 1965
   B. the Civil Rights Act of 1960
   C. the Civil Rights Act of 1957
   D. the 19th Amendment

____ 8. Which are a major source of information on voter behavior?

   A. studies of political socialization
   B. polls
   C. results of specific elections
   D. all of the above

____ 9. The gender gap refers to

   A. a comparison of the numbers of male to female voters.
   B. split-ticket voting.
   C. the differences in the voting patterns of men and women.
   D. loyalty to a political party.

____ 10. Which of the following is a psychological factor that influences voting behavior?

   A. income
   B. education
   C. party identification
   D. family

The Electoral Process

SECTION 1 *THE NOMINATING PROCESS*

◼ TEXT SUMMARY

Nomination—the selecting of candidates for office—is a critical step in the American democratic system. It precedes the **general election,** when voters select the officeholders.

In the United States, nominations are made in five ways. By self-announcement, a person who wants to run for office simply announces the fact. Nominations may also be made in a **caucus,** or a group of like-minded people. Another option is nominating at a convention, or a meeting of the party's members.

Most States now nominate candidates through a **direct primary**—an election held within a party to pick its candidates—of which there are multiple kinds. In **closed primaries,** generally only registered party members may vote. In **open** **primaries,** any voter may vote in one party's primary. Until 2000 when it was ruled unconstitutional, three States used a **blanket primary,** in which voters could choose among all contenders, regardless of party. In some States a candidate must get more than half the votes to win a primary. If no candidate does, the two top vote-getters hold a **runoff primary** to determine the winner. In most States, nearly all elected school and municipal offices are filled through **nonpartisan elections,** in which candidates are not identified by party. Also common is nomination by petition, by which a candidate gets a certain number of qualified voters to sign a petition.

THE **BIG** IDEA

The nominating process is a key part of an election because it narrows the field of possible candidates.

◼ GRAPHIC SUMMARY: *Five Ways to Nominate Candidates*

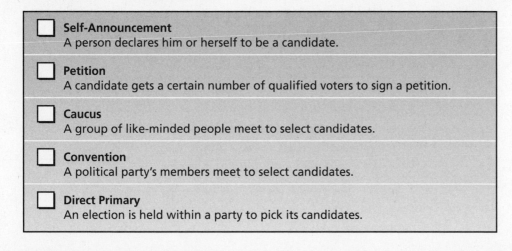

☐ **Self-Announcement**
A person declares him or herself to be a candidate.

☐ **Petition**
A candidate gets a certain number of qualified voters to sign a petition.

☐ **Caucus**
A group of like-minded people meet to select candidates.

☐ **Convention**
A political party's members meet to select candidates.

☐ **Direct Primary**
An election is held within a party to pick its candidates.

Candidates in most States are now nominated in direct primaries.

◼ REVIEW QUESTIONS

1. At what point do voters select officeholders?

2. Chart Skills What is the difference between a convention and a caucus?

TEXT SUMMARY

While the election process is largely governed by State law, federal law regulates the dates and some other aspects of both presidential and congressional elections.

Most States hold elections for State offices on the same day Congress has set for national elections: the Tuesday after the first Monday in November of even-numbered years. **Absentee voting,** or voting by those unable to get to their regular polling places, is usually allowed. Some States allow early voting—casting ballots over a period of days before an election.

A **precinct** is a voting district. A **polling place,** the place where voters actually vote, is located somewhere in or near a precinct. A **ballot** is the device by which voters register their choices in an election. States require that ballots be secret—that no one may see them but the voter.

Most States use a form called the Australian ballot. It is printed at public expense; lists the names of all candidates in an election; is given out only at the polls, one to each voter; and is marked in secret. An office-group ballot lists candidates in a group by office, while a party-column ballot lists them by party. The **coattail effect** occurs when a strong candidate running for an office at the top of a ballot attracts voters to other candidates on the party's ticket.

THE BIG IDEA

The detailed procedures that govern the casting of votes for elected officials help ensure a democratic way of life.

GRAPHIC SUMMARY: *Election Procedures*

The Basics of Election Procedure

- Elections are largely governed by State law.
- Aspects of national elections such as dates are governed by federal law.
- Voting takes place in voting districts called precincts.
- Within the precincts, voters cast their votes at polling places.
- A ballot is used to register a person's votes.
- Most States use a form of the Australian ballot—either an office-group ballot or a party-column ballot.

Election procedures are clearly established by State law and, in some regards, federal law as well.

REVIEW QUESTIONS

1. What is a ballot?

2. **Diagram Skills** Which division of government controls most aspects of elections?

MONEY AND ELECTIONS

■ TEXT SUMMARY

Money plays a key role in politics, but it presents serious problems to democratic governments. The amount of money spent in races varies, but presidential campaigns collect and spend the most.

Parties and their candidates draw their money from two basic sources. Most campaign money comes from private sources, including individuals, families, candidates themselves, and **political action committees (PACs).** PACs are the political arms of special-interest groups. Presidential candidates receive public **subsidies,** which are grants of money from federal and/or State treasuries.

Federal campaign laws are administered by the Federal Election Commission (FEC). These laws apply only to presidential and congressional elections. They require timely disclosure of campaign finance data and limit campaign contributions. Loopholes in campaign finance laws allow candidates to avoid some rules. For instance, federal law neither limits nor requires the reporting of **soft money,** or money given to State and local party organizations for such "party-building activities" as voter registration or party mailings and advertisements. Money that is subject to reporting requirements and amount limits is called **hard money.**

THE **BIG** IDEA

The use of money, a needed campaign resource that poses a variety of problems, is regulated in today's elections.

■ GRAPHIC SUMMARY: *Political Campaign Money*

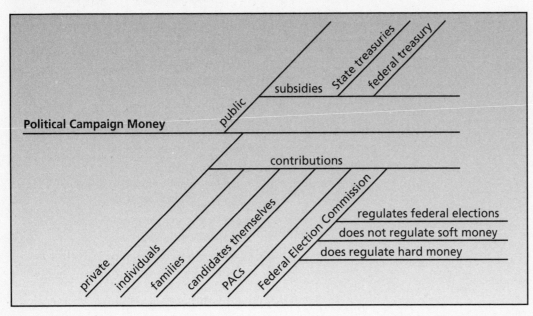

Campaign money comes from both public and private sources and is regulated by the Federal Election Commission.

■ REVIEW QUESTIONS

1. Is hard money or soft money subject to reporting requirements?

2. Diagram Skills Who gives public subsidies to campaigns?

Name _____ Class _____ Date _____

CHAPTER 7 *Test*

IDENTIFYING MAIN IDEAS

Write the letter of the correct answer in the blank provided. (10 points each)

____ 1. The nominating process

    A. chooses new government officeholders.
    B. selects political-party leaders.
    C. narrows the field of possible candidates for an election.
    D. all of the above

____ 2. Voters select government officials during the

    A. convention.
    B. general election.
    C. primary election.
    D. political action committee.

____ 3. Most nominations today are made by

    A. self-announcement.
    B. caucus.
    C. convention.
    D. direct primaries.

____ 4. In a closed primary,

    A. any voter may vote in any one party's primary.
    B. voters may choose any candidates regardless of their parties.
    C. candidates are not identified by party.
    D. generally only registered party members may vote.

____ 5. The election process is largely governed by

    A. State law.
    B. federal law.
    C. local law.
    D. PACs.

____ 6. Congress has set the day for national elections as

    A. the Monday after the third Tuesday in November in even-numbered years.
    B. the Tuesday after the first Monday in November in even-numbered years.
    C. the Monday after the first Tuesday in May in even-numbered years.
    D. the Tuesday after the first Monday in November in odd-numbered years.

____ 7. The place at which voters actually vote is a

    A. caucus.
    B. convention.
    C. precinct.
    D. polling place.

____ 8. An Australian ballot

    A. is printed at the public's expense.
    B. lists the names of all candidates.
    C. is given out only at the polls.
    D. all of the above

____ 9. Which of the following is an example of soft money?

    A. money given to a major party's presidential candidate
    B. money given to a minority party's senatorial candidate
    C. a small campaign contribution from a college student
    D. money given to a major party for a television ad about the party's goals

____ 10. Federal campaign laws apply to

    A. presidential and congressional elections only.
    B. all elections.
    C. elections with campaign spending above certain levels.
    D. PAC contributions.

46 **CHAPTER 7** *Guide to the Essentials* © Prentice-Hall, Inc.

Mass Media and Public Opinion

CHAPTER 8

SECTION 1 THE FORMATION OF PUBLIC OPINION

■ TEXT SUMMARY

Public opinion refers to the attitudes of a significant number of people about **public affairs,** or matters of government and politics that concern the people at large. Political socialization is the process by which people learn ideas and develop opinions about issues. Many factors play a part in this process.

Family and education are two of the most important factors in political socialization. Children pick up fundamental attitudes from their families. Schools teach children the value of the American political system and train them to become good citizens.

Other important factors in developing political opinions include occupation and race. Additionally, the **mass media—** those means of communication that

reach many people simultaneously, such as newspapers, television, and the Internet—have a huge effect on the formation of public opinion.

Peer groups are the groups of people with whom one regularly associates, including friends, neighbors, classmates, and co-workers. Members of peer groups usually share political opinions.

Public opinions are also affected by the views expressed by **opinion leaders**— those people who can strongly influence the views of others. Historic events, such as wars, affect people's lives and thus can also influence public opinion.

> ### THE **BIG** IDEA
>
> Several factors, including family and education, help to shape a person's opinions about public affairs.

■ GRAPHIC SUMMARY: *Factors That Shape Public Opinion*

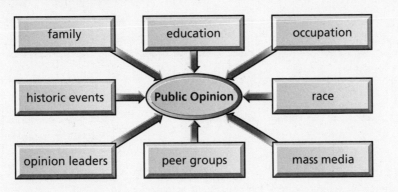

Many factors play a part in shaping public opinion.

■ REVIEW QUESTIONS

1. What is public opinion?

2. **Diagram Skills** List three factors that influence public opinion.

MEASURING PUBLIC OPINION

TEXT SUMMARY

Government leaders make policy based on public opinion. Of the many ways to measure public opinion, some are more accurate than others.

A winning party and candidate often claim to have a **mandate,** or instructions from the constituency. Based on this they say that election results indicate public opinion, but few candidates receive true mandates. **Interest groups,** or private organizations that work to shape public policy, often present their views as public opinion, but how many people they represent is unknown. Public officials can use the media and public contacts to gain some sense of public opinion.

The best measures of public opinion are **public opinion polls,** or devices that collect information through questioning. **Straw votes,** which ask the same question to many people, are not reliable because those who respond may not represent the total population.

Scientific polling, which can be very accurate, breaks the polling process into steps. First, choose the "universe," that is, the population the poll aims to measure. Then get a **sample**—a representative slice of the universe. Most pollsters will draw a **random sample,** or one in which members of the chosen universe are equally likely to be picked. Some polls use the less reliable **quota sample,** one that deliberately reflects several of the major characteristics of a given universe. Next pollsters prepare valid questions, select and control the polling process, and report the results.

THE **BIG** IDEA

Of the methods for measuring public opinion, polls are the most effective.

GRAPHIC SUMMARY: *Measuring Public Opinion*

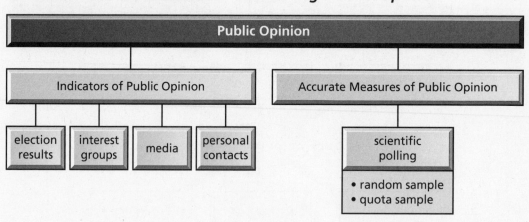

Scientific polling is an accurate way of learning public opinion.

REVIEW QUESTIONS

1. List the steps in scientific polling.

2. Diagram Skills What are the four indicators of public opinion?

THE MASS MEDIA

TEXT SUMMARY

A **medium** is a means of communication; *media* is the word's plural. The American public gets information about public issues through several forms of mass media.

Four major mass media are particularly important in American politics. Television has the most influence, followed by newspapers, radio, and magazines. Other media, such as books and the Internet, also have an impact.

The media play a large part in setting the **public agenda,** or the public issues that people think and talk about. The media also have a central role in elections. For example, television has reduced the importance of political parties. In the past, candidates relied on their party members to reach the voters. Now, because television allows the candidates to reach the public directly, many candidates operate with only loose ties to a party. They work hard to get good media coverage and to provide the media with good **sound bites**—focused, snappy statements that can be aired in 35 or 45 seconds.

The influence of the media is limited in some ways. Few people actually follow political issues carefully in the media. Also, those who do tend to watch, listen to, or read choose favorite sources rather than sources with contrary opinions to their own. For example, many Democrats do not watch the televised campaign appearances of Republican candidates, and vice versa.

THE BIG IDEA

The media are our most important sources of political information.

GRAPHIC SUMMARY: *The Mass Media*

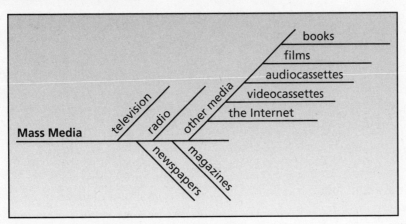

The many forms of mass media greatly impact American politics.

REVIEW QUESTIONS

1. How do the media affect the public agenda?

2. Diagram Skills What are the four forms of the media with the greatest impact on politics?

Guide to the Essentials **CHAPTER 8**

CHAPTER 8 *Test*

▣ IDENTIFYING MAIN IDEAS

Write the letter of the correct answer in the blank provided. (10 points each)

____ 1. Public opinion refers to

A. the process through which people form opinions about issues.

B. the attitudes held by large numbers of Americans.

C. private organizations that work to change public policy.

D. a person who influences how others think.

____ 2. Which are the most important factors in political socialization?

A. family and education

B. race and occupation

C. peer groups and opinion leaders

D. mass media and historic events

____ 3. A popular movie star who speaks publicly about a political issue may become

A. an opinion leader.

B. a pollster.

C. a random sample.

D. a mandate.

____ 4. A candidate's victory in an election is sometimes interpreted by him or her as

A. a representative sample.

B. a medium.

C. a sound bite.

D. a mandate.

____ 5. If you asked the same question about an upcoming election to many people, you would be conducting a

A. scientific poll.

B. straw vote.

C. public agenda.

D. representative sample.

____ 6. The most accurate way to measure public opinion is by

A. election results.

B. straw votes.

C. studying the media.

D. scientific polling.

____ 7. Which of the following is not part of the mass media?

A. newspapers

B. books

C. the Internet

D. music CDs

____ 8. Which of the mass media has the most impact on American politics?

A. radio

B. television

C. movies

D. the Internet

____ 9. How has television affected political campaigns?

A. It has led to less coverage of issues.

B. It has made candidates use more polls.

C. It has made candidates less dependent on political parties.

D. It has made the public less interested in elections.

____ 10. The public agenda refers to

A. the goal of a mandate.

B. the political stance of an opinion leader.

C. the public issues people think and talk about.

D. the objective of an interest group.

Interest Groups

SECTION 1 — THE NATURE OF INTEREST GROUPS

▌ TEXT SUMMARY

An **interest group** is a private organization whose members share views. It tries to promote its interests by influencing **public policy,** or the goals a government sets and the actions it takes to meet them. Interest groups work at the federal, State, and local levels.

Interest groups and political parties both exist for political purposes, but their goals differ. Political parties care mostly about *who* takes part in government, while interest groups care mostly about *what* the government does—especially on certain issues.

The role of interest groups in politics is controversial. In their favor, they stimulate interest in **public affairs,** or issues that concern the people at large. They offer people a chance to participate in politics and find others who may not live near them but who do share their views. They often provide useful information to the government, while also keeping close tabs on it. Since they compete with one another, interest groups often limit each other's extremes.

Interest groups are criticized for having more influence than they deserve based on the worth of their causes or the number of people they represent. It can be hard to tell how many people an interest group represents. Some interest groups do not represent the views of all the people for whom they claim to speak. Finally, some interest groups do engage in dishonest behavior.

> ### THE **BIG** IDEA
>
> Interest groups offer Americans an important means of influencing U.S. public policy.

▌ GRAPHIC SUMMARY: *Are Interest Groups Good or Bad?*

Interest Groups	
Positives	**Negatives**
1. help stimulate interest in public affairs	1. can have more influence than they deserve
2. are based on shared views, not shared geography	2. difficult to figure out how many people they represent
3. provide information to government	3. some do not represent the views of all the people for whom they claim to speak
4. keep tabs on government	4. some engage in dishonest behavior
5. can limit each other's extremes	

The political power of interest groups is viewed both positively and negatively.

▌ REVIEW QUESTIONS

1. What is an interest group?

2. Chart Skills Name two positive contributions of interest groups.

SECTION 2 TYPES OF INTEREST GROUPS

◼ TEXT SUMMARY

Many Americans belong to several organizations that meet the definition of an interest group. Such groups may be very large or quite small. Most interest groups represent economic—that is, income-earning—interests, such as business, labor, agriculture, and professionals.

A **trade association** is an interest group formed by one segment of the business community, such as banking. A **labor union** is an interest group whose members are workers who hold similar jobs or work in the same industry, such as police officers.

An influential set of interest groups focuses on agriculture. These groups may represent farmers who raise particular commodities. Some professional interest groups also carry weight in American politics. The largest of these are organizations of physicians, lawyers, and teachers.

Other interest groups are devoted to specific political and social causes. They promote groups such as veterans and elderly people, or political causes such as protection of the environment. Still other interest groups promote certain religious interests. **Public-interest groups** work for "the public good"—that is, they try to represent all the people in the country on particular issues, such as voting rights. They usually focus on issues that affect the roles that all Americans share, such as citizen, consumer, or drinker of water.

THE BIG IDEA

Interest groups are formed around many issues, such as public interest and economics.

◼ GRAPHIC SUMMARY: *Types of Interest Groups*

Purpose	Example
to promote business	American Bankers Association
to organize labor	Fraternal Order of Police
to protect agricultural interests	National Farmers Union
to promote professions	American Medical Association
to promote social programs	Veterans of Foreign Wars
for religious purposes	American Jewish Congress
for the public good	League of Women Voters

Interest groups work for an array of public policies that benefit their members.

◼ REVIEW QUESTIONS

1. Who do labor unions represent?

2. **Chart Skills** What is the purpose of the National Farmers Union?

SECTION 3 INTEREST GROUPS AT WORK

TEXT SUMMARY

Interest groups reach out to the public for three purposes. First, they supply the public with information in an effort to gain support for their causes. Second, they work to build positive images for their groups. Third, they promote the public policies they favor.

To achieve their goals, interest groups often use **propaganda**—a technique of persuasion aimed at influencing individual or group behaviors to create certain beliefs. These beliefs may be true, false, or partly true.

Interest groups recognize the role of political parties in selecting policy-makers and thus try to influence their behavior. Some interest groups form political action committees (PACs) to raise campaign funds for candidates whom they think will further their goals.

Single-interest groups are PACs that concentrate their efforts on one issue. They work for or against a political candidate based only on his or her stand on that one issue.

Interest groups may engage in **lobbying,** or bringing group pressure to bear on all aspects of the making of public policy. Lobbyists, or agents for interest groups, use many techniques in their work, including **grass roots** pressure, or organized pressure from the average voters. To prevent corruption, federal and State laws regulate lobbyists' activities.

THE BIG IDEA

Interest groups use propaganda, form political action committees, and engage lobbyists in order to influence public policy.

GRAPHIC SUMMARY: Techniques Used by Interest Groups

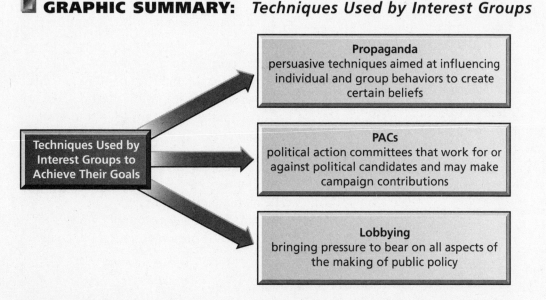

Interest groups use various techniques to influence public opinion, political parties, and the making of public policy.

REVIEW QUESTIONS

1. How do single-interest groups decide whether or not to support a political candidate?

2. **Diagram Skills** On what process does lobbying put pressure?

CHAPTER 9 *Test*

▧ IDENTIFYING MAIN IDEAS

Write the letter of the correct answer in the blank provided. (10 points each)

_____ 1. An interest group is a private organization that forms to

   A. support elections at the local level.
   B. promote the interests of its members.
   C. nominate candidates for public office.
   D. measure public opinion.

_____ 2. What is public policy?

   A. issues that concern the public at large
   B. policy set by the people rather than the government
   C. a government's goals and actions
   D. a technique of influencing public opinion

_____ 3. A positive activity of interest groups is to

   A. get people interested in public affairs.
   B. provide information to government.
   C. join together people from different parts of the country.
   D. all of the above

_____ 4. Interest groups are often criticized for

   A. engaging in dishonest behavior.
   B. answering only to their members.
   C. working too independently of each other.
   D. working at all levels of government.

_____ 5. The American Bankers Association is an example of a

   A. labor union.
   B. public-interest group.
   C. trade association.
   D. single-interest group.

_____ 6. Which is an economic interest that is represented by most interest groups?

   A. business interests
   B. agricultural interests
   C. professional interests
   D. all of the above

_____ 7. A single-interest group

   A. works to elect or defeat candidates based on several factors, including experience.
   B. concentrates on electing or defeating candidates based on one issue.
   C. does not engage in lobbying.
   D. works for the public good.

_____ 8. A lobbyist encourages parents to write letters to their representatives in Congress in support of an education bill. This is an example of

   A. grass-roots pressure.
   B. PAC contributions.
   C. a public-interest group.
   D. propaganda.

_____ 9. A political action committee's purpose is to

   A. use propaganda.
   B. work for the interests of all Americans.
   C. raise money for political candidates.
   D. encourage Americans to join interest groups.

_____ 10. Lobbyists' activities are

   A. illegal.
   B. regulated by laws.
   C. not concerned with public policy.
   D. driven by personal, not group, goals.

Congress

SECTION 1

THE NATIONAL LEGISLATURE

TEXT SUMMARY

Congress is the branch of the National Government that makes laws. The Constitution says that Congress will be bicameral—that is, made up of two houses, which are the Senate and the House of Representatives. Congress is bicameral in order to give fair representation to both large and small States. In the Senate, each State is represented equally and has equal power. In the House of Representatives, States with larger populations get more representation.

The **term** of Congress is the length of time its officials serve after their election. Each term begins on January 3 of every odd-numbered year and lasts for two years.

Congress holds one **session**, or meeting period, every year. Each term has two sessions. Congress can **adjourn**, or end, a session when it finishes its business. Today, Congress meets almost year-round, with several recesses, or breaks. The President has an as yet unused power to **prorogue**, or adjourn, a session if the two houses cannot agree on an adjournment date.

In case of an emergency, the President may call Congress into **special session.** Because Congress spends so much of the year in session, the President has not called a special session in over 50 years.

THE **BIG** IDEA

Congress, made up of the Senate and the House of Representatives, is the National Government's legislative branch.

GRAPHIC SUMMARY: *Representation in Congress*

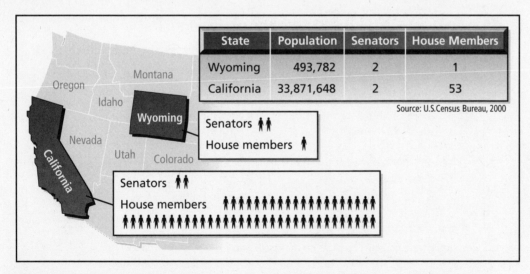

State	Population	Senators	House Members
Wyoming	493,782	2	1
California	33,871,648	2	53

Source: U.S. Census Bureau, 2000

California has many more representatives in the House than Wyoming does, but both States have two senators.

REVIEW QUESTIONS

1. When does Congress start each new term?

2. **Diagram Skills** How does California's representation in Congress differ from Wyoming's?

THE HOUSE OF REPRESENTATIVES

◼ TEXT SUMMARY

Today the House of Representatives has 435 members. Congress **apportions,** or distributes, the House's seats among the States according to their populations. Each State sends at least one representative to the House.

Every ten years the House's seats are **reapportioned**—redistributed—when the United States counts its population. This count is called a census. After each census has been conducted, the number of representatives of any State may change based on changes in its population.

Once Congress tells each State how many House seats it has, the State draws the boundaries of its electoral districts. States must follow guidelines and avoid **gerrymandering,** or drawing districts

in a way that is advantageous to the State legislature's controlling party.

Since 1842, the use of the **single-member district** arrangement has allowed the voters of each congressional district to choose one representative from a pool of candidates associated with that district. Before 1842, voters in some States chose their representatives **at-large,** or from the State as a whole.

To become a representative, a person must be at least 25 years of age, have been a citizen of the United States for seven years, and live in the State that he or she wishes to represent. Representatives serve two-year terms and may be elected an unlimited number of times. Congressional elections are held in November of even-numbered years. An **off-year election** is a congressional election that is held between presidential elections.

THE BIG IDEA

Members of the House, who serve an unlimited number of two-year terms, represent districts of roughly equal populations.

◼ GRAPHIC SUMMARY: *Reapportionment*

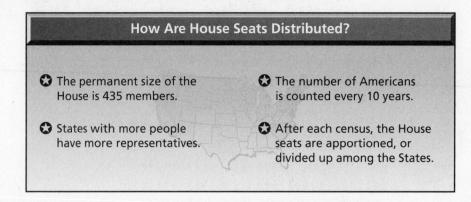

How Are House Seats Distributed?

✪ The permanent size of the House is 435 members.

✪ The number of Americans is counted every 10 years.

✪ States with more people have more representatives.

✪ After each census, the House seats are apportioned, or divided up among the States.

Congress periodically reapportions its seats so that each State is represented fairly.

◼ REVIEW QUESTIONS

1. Describe the single-member district arrangement of selecting a representative.

2. Diagram Skills What is the basis for apportioning House seats?

THE SENATE

◼ TEXT SUMMARY

The Senate has 100 members, two from each State—a number established by the Constitution. The Senate is therefore a much smaller body than the House of Representatives. The voters of each State elect one senator in any given election, unless the other seat has been vacated by death, resignation, or expulsion and so also needs to be filled.

The Senate is called the "upper house" of Congress because senators meet stricter qualifications and serve longer terms than representatives do. Senators serve six-year terms whose start dates are staggered so that only one-third of the senators' terms end at the same time. This means that every two years about 33 senators come up for reelection. The Senate is, therefore, a **continuous body:** it never contains only new members, so a majority of its membership always has experience.

The longer terms for senators and the larger size and geographic diversity of their **constituencies**—those people who elect them—are designed to remove senators, at least somewhat, from day-to-day politics. In contrast to their **colleagues,** or coworkers, in the House, senators have more power and prestige and are more likely to be seen as national political leaders.

To become a senator, a person must be at least 30 years of age, have been a citizen of the United States for at least nine years, and live in the State that he or she wishes to represent.

THE BIG IDEA

Each State has two seats in the Senate, the smaller of the two houses of Congress.

◼ GRAPHIC SUMMARY: *Membership in Congress*

Who Can Become a Member of Congress?		
Qualification	*House*	*Senate*
Age	At least 25	At least 30
Citizenship	At least 7 years	At least 9 years
Residency	Must be from the state	Must be from the state

The qualifications for senator are harder to meet than those for representative.

◼ REVIEW QUESTIONS

1. What makes the Senate a continuous body?

2. Chart Skills What is the youngest age at which a person may become a member of Congress?

 **SECTION 4**

THE MEMBERS OF CONGRESS

■ TEXT SUMMARY

Most members of Congress are white, upper-middle class, and male, although more women and minorities have been elected in recent years. Most also have previous political experience, such as being a State governor or legislator.

Typically, the members of Congress take on one of the following roles as they vote on bills. As **trustees,** they consider each bill's merits, regardless of the views of constituents. As delegates, they base their votes on the wishes of the "folks back home," their constituents. As **partisans,** they vote in line with their political party. As **politicos,** they consider all of these factors when they vote.

On committees, members of Congress screen proposed bills and decide which should be acted on. Committees also exercise the **oversight function,** checking that the executive branch is working effectively and in line with the policies that Congress has set.

Members of Congress also act as servants of their constituents. Through this duty they help those they represent solve problems with the National Government.

In performing the above roles, members of Congress carry out five key duties: they act as legislators, representatives of their constituents, committee members, servants of their constituents, and politicians. For their work, they receive a salary and benefits such as the **franking privilege,** the right to send mail postage-free.

> ### THE **BIG** IDEA
>
> **Members of Congress, who receive generous pay and good benefits, fulfill various roles.**

■ GRAPHIC SUMMARY: *Duties of Members of Congress*

Legislator
Makes laws

Committee Member
Screens bills

Oversees the executive branch's enforcement of laws

Constituent Representative
Represents/votes as "folks back home" want

Constituent Servant
Does favors for citizens

Politician
Keeps in touch with party leaders and constituents back home

Members of Congress have many duties beyond making laws.

■ REVIEW QUESTIONS

1. Name four roles members of Congress can take on when voting on a bill.

2. Chart Skills What is different about being a constituent representative and a constituent servant?

Name _____ Class _____ Date _____

CHAPTER 10 *Test*

◼ IDENTIFYING MAIN IDEAS

Write the letter of the correct answer in the blank provided. (10 points each)

____ **1.** How long is a term in the House of Representatives?

  A. 1 year
  B. 2 years
  C. 4 years
  D. 6 years

____ **2.** The number of House members representing each State is recalculated every

  A. 2 years.
  B. 4 years.
  C. 6 years.
  D. 10 years.

____ **3.** When Congress adjourns, it

  A. ends a session.
  B. decides whether to consider a bill.
  C. breaks into committees.
  D. discusses an emergency situation.

____ **4.** What does it mean to *reapportion* seats in the House of Representatives?

  A. House districts are changed based on election results.
  B. Newly elected representatives take their seats in the House.
  C. The number of House seats for each State is changed based on population changes.
  D. One term of Congress ends and a new one begins.

____ **5.** A House district drawn to give an advantage to one political party is

  A. an off-year election.
  B. a single-member district.
  C. a gerrymander.
  D. a census.

____ **6.** How many senators are up for re-election every two years?

  A. one-sixth
  B. one-third
  C. one-half
  D. all

____ **7.** Because a majority of senators are always experienced, the Senate is said to be

  A. a house of colleagues.
  B. a continuous body.
  C. bicameral.
  D. a partisan body.

____ **8.** In the role of servant to their constituents, members of Congress

  A. work for their political party.
  B. oversee the work of the executive branch.
  C. screen bills for action by the whole House or Senate.
  D. help people from their district or State deal with the National Government.

____ **9.** A member of Congress who votes based on the wishes of his or her constituents operates in which of the following roles?

  A. trustee
  B. delegate
  C. partisan
  D. politico

____ **10.** To run for Senate, a person must be at least how old?

  A. 21
  B. 30
  C. 45
  D. 25

Powers of Congress

SECTION 1 — THE SCOPE OF CONGRESSIONAL POWERS

■ TEXT SUMMARY

Article 1 of the Constitution describes Congress and grants it specific powers, which are called **expressed powers.** The Constitution also states the powers denied to Congress. Those powers of Congress not listed in the Constitution but needed to carry out its expressed powers are **implied powers.** It also has **inherent powers** by its very nature as a national government's legislative branch.

Arguments about Congress's power began with the writing of the Constitution. The **strict constructionists** wanted the States to keep as much power as possible. They believed that the best government is

one that governs least. Congress should use only its expressed powers and the implied powers needed to carry out its duties.

The **liberal constructionists** wanted a broad, or liberal, interpretation of the powers of Congress. They believed that a good government is an active one. Early on, the liberal constructionists won out. Congress has since acquired more powers than the Framers could ever have imagined.

Events such as wars and economic crises have contributed to the growth of national power. So also have improvements in communication and transportation. Americans have generally agreed with, or come to **consensus** about, the scope of powers assumed by Congress.

> ### THE **BIG** IDEA
>
> The Constitution gives Congress certain powers, but liberal interpretation has given Congress great scope.

■ GRAPHIC SUMMARY: *Strict v. Liberal Constructionists*

Americans came to a consensus that favored a liberal construction of the Constitution.

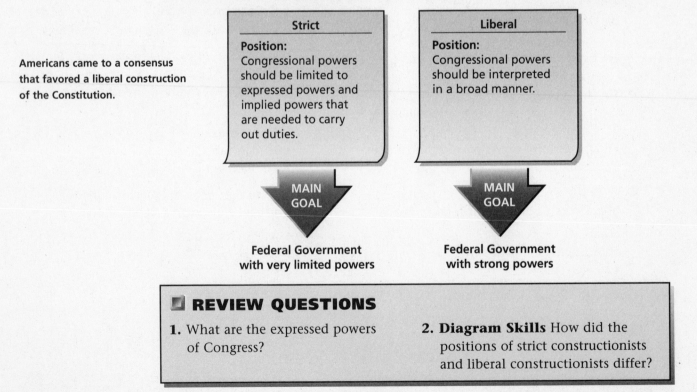

Strict	Liberal
Position: Congressional powers should be limited to expressed powers and implied powers that are needed to carry out duties.	**Position:** Congressional powers should be interpreted in a broad manner.
MAIN GOAL	MAIN GOAL
Federal Government with very limited powers	Federal Government with strong powers

■ REVIEW QUESTIONS

1. What are the expressed powers of Congress?

2. Diagram Skills How did the positions of strict constructionists and liberal constructionists differ?

THE EXPRESSED POWERS OF MONEY AND COMMERCE

◼ TEXT SUMMARY

The Constitution gives Congress the power to **tax**—to impose a charge on people or property in order to fund public needs. Tax collecting must, however, be used in accord with all other provisions of the Constitution.

Over 90 percent of the revenue of the Federal Government comes from taxes, of which there are two kinds. **Direct taxes** are paid directly by the taxed person. Income tax is a direct tax. **Indirect taxes** are first paid by one person, such as a manufacturer, and are then passed on to others, such as consumers.

The Constitution allows Congress to borrow money. Until quite recently, the Federal Government spent more than it took in each year and borrowed to make up the difference. This practice, called **deficit financing,** led to a very large **public debt**, or money owed by the nation. In recent years, the government has achieved a balanced budget.

Congress's **commerce power** allows it to regulate trade, or interstate and foreign business. The Supreme Court has ruled that "trade" includes transportation and other ways in which people interact. However, Congress may not tax exports or favor one State over another.

Only Congress has the power to "coin money." Money made by the government is called **legal tender,** or money that by law must be accepted in payment of debts.

Congress may also make laws about **bankruptcy.** A bankrupt person is one a court finds to be unable to pay his or her bills. Bankruptcy is the legal process by which this person's assets are divided among those owed.

THE **BIG** IDEA

Many of the expressed powers of Congress have to do with money and commerce or business.

◼ GRAPHIC SUMMARY: *Congress's Expressed Powers of Money and Commerce*

Money	Commerce
• Tax • Spend • Coin Money • Borrow Money • Set Bankruptcy Laws	• Regulate Interstate Commerce • Regulate International Trade

Congress has great power to regulate money and business.

◼ REVIEW QUESTIONS

1. What is the difference between a direct tax and an indirect tax?

2. Chart Skills What powers related to money does Congress have?

 # OTHER EXPRESSED POWERS

■ TEXT SUMMARY

Eight of Congress's expressed powers deal with war and national defense. Congress shares these powers with the President, who is commander in chief of all the country's armed forces. Only Congress, however, has the power to declare war. It can also organize and support an army and navy.

Among its other expressed powers, Congress makes laws about **naturalization,** or the process by which foreigners become U.S. citizens. Congress can also establish post offices. Congress has used this power to pass laws against crimes involving the postal system.

The Constitution asks Congress to promote science and the arts by protecting the work of both writers and inventors. Congress has done this, in part, through copyright laws. A **copyright** is the exclusive right of an author to reproduce, publish, and sell his or her work. A **patent** gives an inventor the sole right to make, use, or sell "any new and useful art, machine, manufacture, . . . or any new and useful improvement."

Congress has the power to fix standards for weights and measures for the country. It may also acquire, manage, and sell certain federal lands, such as parks. The Federal Government may take private property by **eminent domain,** or the power to take private land for public use. Congress also has the power to set up federal courts lower than the Supreme Court.

THE BIG IDEA

Congress has a number of major expressed powers that are not related to money and commerce.

■ GRAPHIC SUMMARY: *Expressed Powers of Congress*

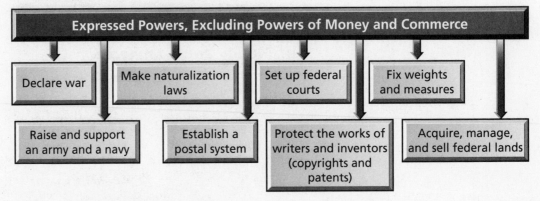

Many of the expressed powers of Congress affect the daily lives of Americans.

■ REVIEW QUESTIONS

1. What is the purpose of copyrights and patents?

2. Diagram Skills What power of Congress ensures that a gallon measure is the same in each State?

THE IMPLIED POWERS

■ TEXT SUMMARY

Congress's implied powers come from the Constitution's **Necessary and Proper Clause.** This clause grants Congress all the powers "necessary and proper" for executing its expressed powers. The clause is also called the "Elastic Clause" because its use has greatly stretched Congress's powers. For example, although the Constitution says nothing about education, Congress **appropriates,** or assigns to a particular use, billions of dollars for education every year.

The battle over implied powers began in the 1790s. Liberal constructionists led by Alexander Hamilton wanted Congress to set up a national bank. To do so was not an expressed power; the liberal constructionists saw it as an implied power.

Strict constructionists led by Thomas Jefferson thought that the government should use only those powers *absolutely* necessary to carry out the expressed powers. However, the liberal constructionists won out.

In 1819, the Supreme Court heard the case *McCulloch* v. *Maryland*, which hinged on the constitutionality of Congress's power to set up a national bank. The Supreme Court ruled that the bank was constitutional, therefore supporting the idea of implied powers. Since that time, the **doctrine,** or fundamental policy, of implied powers has been applied continually.

THE **BIG** IDEA

The Necessary and Proper Clause led to massive expansion of Congress's power.

■ GRAPHIC SUMMARY: *The Implied Powers of Congress*

The expressed power	implies the power
to lay and collect taxes	• to create tax laws and punish tax evaders • to use tax revenues to fund welfare, public schools, health and housing programs • to require States to meet certain conditions to qualify for federal funding
to borrow money	• to establish the Federal Reserve System of banks
to establish naturalization law	• to regulate and limit immigration
to raise armies and a navy	• to draft Americans into the military
to regulate commerce	• to establish a minimum wage • to ban discrimination in workplaces and public facilities • to pass laws protecting the disabled • to regulate banking
to establish post offices	• to prohibit mail fraud and obstruction of the mails • to bar the shipping of certain items through the mails

The implied powers of Congress are those that are reasonably assumed based on the expressed powers in the Constitution.

■ REVIEW QUESTIONS

1. Why is the Necessary and Proper Clause often called the "Elastic Clause"?

2. Chart Skills From what power is the implied power to limit immigration drawn?

 # THE NONLEGISLATIVE POWERS

TEXT SUMMARY

The Constitution gives Congress a number of nonlegislative powers. For instance, Congress may propose constitutional amendments by a two-thirds vote in each of its houses.

Congress also has certain rarely used electoral duties. The House may elect a President if no candidate wins a majority of electoral votes. The Senate may choose a Vice President in similar circumstances. If the office of Vice President becomes vacant, the President nominates a **successor,** or replacement, who is subject to a vote in Congress.

The Constitution says that any civil officer, such as the President, can be removed from office. The House has the power to **impeach,** or bring charges against, the officer. Charges may be brought against someone for actions such as **perjury**, or lying under oath, and the failure to respond to a **subpoena,** which is a court order to appear in court or to produce requested materials.

The Senate serves as judge for the trial. The Senate can vote to **acquit,** or find the officer not guilty. In such a case, members of Congress can try to **censure** the official, that is to issue a formal condemnation of his or her actions.

The Senate also has certain executive powers. It can advise the executive branch. It has the power to approve appointments and treaties made by the President.

Lastly, Congress has the power to investigate any matter that falls within the scope of its powers. Congress uses its standing committees to do this.

THE BIG IDEA

Congress has a number of nonlegislative powers, including electoral, executive, and investigative powers.

GRAPHIC SUMMARY: *Nonlegislative Powers of Congress*

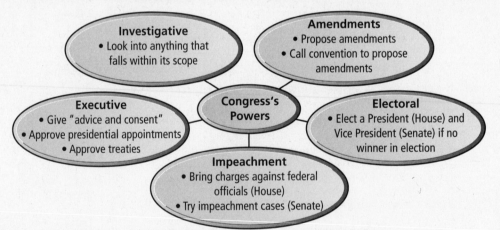

Congress's nonlegislative powers sometimes result in dramatic investigations and hearings.

REVIEW QUESTIONS

1. What occurs in an impeachment?

2. **Diagram Skills** What are the electoral powers of Congress?

CHAPTER 11 *Test*

IDENTIFYING MAIN IDEAS

Write the letter of the correct answer in the blank provided. (10 points each)

____ 1. The expressed powers of Congress are

    A. implied in the Constitution.
    B. those that it assumes in times of crisis.
    C. stated directly in the Constitution.
    D. given to it by the Supreme Court.

____ 2. The consensus of American opinion favors

    A. strict interpretation of the Constitution.
    B. neutral interpretation of the Constitution.
    C. no regard for the Constitution.
    D. liberal interpretation of the Constitution.

____ 3. The commerce power of Congress allows it to

    A. regulate trade and business.
    B. set rules for naturalization.
    C. set up federal courts.
    D. borrow money.

____ 4. The power that allows Congress to take private property for such uses as an interstate highway system or a national park is

    A. the commerce power.
    B. the power of eminent domain.
    C. the borrowing power.
    D. the power to tax.

____ 5. The exclusive legal right an author has to his or her own work is protected by

    A. a patent.
    B. a copyright.
    C. legal tender.
    D. bankruptcy.

____ 6. A store must accept U.S. dollar bills in payment because the dollar bill is

    A. a direct tax.
    B. an indirect tax.
    C. legal tender.
    D. eminent domain.

____ 7. The power of the House of Representatives to officially charge an official with wrongdoing is the power of

    A. impeachment.
    B. perjury.
    C. subpoena.
    D. censure.

____ 8. If no presidential candidate wins a majority of the electoral votes, the President is chosen in

    A. the Senate.
    B. both houses of Congress.
    C. the Supreme Court.
    D. the House of Representatives.

____ 9. The first battle over the implied powers of Congress was fought over the creation of

    A. an army.
    B. a direct tax.
    C. a national bank.
    D. a patent.

____ 10. Which of the following must approve presidential appointments?

    A. the Senate
    B. the House of Representatives
    C. liberal constructionists
    D. strict constructionists

Congress in Action

SECTION 1 CONGRESS ORGANIZES

▉ TEXT SUMMARY

When Congress starts a new term, the House reorganizes because new members are taking seats. The members elect their leader, who swears in all the members. They then adopt their work rules and appoint the members of their permanent committees. The Senate does not need to reorganize because two-thirds of its members stay the same from term to term.

Presiding over the House is the **Speaker of the House,** who may debate or vote on any matter before the House. The Speaker is the majority party's leader and the most powerful person in Congress.

The Vice President of the United States acts as **president of the Senate.** The Vice President oversees the Senate's sessions but cannot debate and votes only in a tie. In the Vice President's absence, the **president *pro tempore*** presides.

Next to the Speaker, Congress's most powerful leaders are the majority and minority party **floor leaders,** the parties' chief spokespeople. They are selected during the **party caucuses**—meetings of the members of each party just before Congress convenes. The floor leaders help pass laws that their parties want. They are aided by **whips,** or assistant floor leaders.

Committee chairmen are also powerful in Congress. They head the standing committees that do most of Congress's work. Each is almost always that committee's longest-standing member from the majority party. This custom is part of the **seniority rule,** which gives the most important posts in Congress to party members who have served the longest.

THE BIG IDEA

Congress carefully organizes itself to get its complex job done.

▉ GRAPHIC SUMMARY: *Leadership in Congress*

Leaders from the majority party have more power than leaders from the minority party.

House		Senate	
Presiding officer and party leader		**Presiding officers**	
Speaker of the House		President of the Senate	President *Pro Tempore*
Party officers		**Party officers**	
Majority Floor Leader	Minority Floor Leader	Majority Floor Leader	Minority Floor Leader
Majority Whip	Minority Whip	Majority Whip	Minority Whip

▉ REVIEW QUESTIONS

1. How does the seniority rule work?

2. Diagram Skills What two primary roles does the Speaker of the House play?

COMMITTEES IN CONGRESS

TEXT SUMMARY

Congress does most of its work in committees, or small groups. The **standing committees** are permanent, specialize in one subject each, and handle all bills that relate to that subject. The majority party holds a majority of seats on each committee. The parties decide committee membership, and Congress ratifies the choices.

The House Rules Committee is one of the most powerful committees of the House. Its members determine when and under what conditions the whole House will debate and vote on bills. The Rules Committee can speed up, delay, or even prevent action on a bill.

Congress uses several special committees. A **select committee** is a group set up for a specific and usually temporary purpose, such as an investigation. A **joint committee,** which can be either temporary or permanent, includes members from both houses so that separate committees in the houses do not duplicate each other's work. A **conference committee** is a type of temporary joint committee that is set up when the House and Senate have each passed different versions of the same law. The conference committee works out a compromise bill that both houses will accept.

THE BIG IDEA

The Senate and the House both divide into committees to manage their business and decide which bills will receive attention.

GRAPHIC SUMMARY: *Committees of Congress*

Standing Committee	• Permanent • Specializes in one subject • Handles all bills relating to that subject **Examples:** House Rules Committee, House Ways and Means Committee, Senate Armed Services Committee, Senate Finance Committee
Select Committee	• Usually temporary • Set up for a specific purpose, such as an investigation **Examples:** Select Committee on Aging (both houses), Senate Select Committee on Presidential Campaign Activities, House Committee on Agriculture
Joint Committee	• Permanent or temporary • Includes members of both houses so that the houses do not duplicate work **Examples:** Joint Economic Committee, Joint Committee on Printing, Joint Committee on the Library of Congress, Joint Committee on Taxation
Conference Committee	• Temporary • Works out a compromise bill when the House and the Senate have passed different versions of the same bill

To deal with its heavy workload, Congress divides into several types of committees.

REVIEW QUESTIONS

1. What is the major job of the House Rules Committee?

2. Chart Skills Which type of committee would be used to investigate improper usage of the Internet?

HOW A BILL BECOMES A LAW: THE HOUSE

◼ TEXT SUMMARY

Congress considers thousands of bills and resolutions at each session. A **bill** is a proposed law that applies to the nation as a whole or to certain people or places. A **resolution** is a measure that one house passes but that does not have the force of law. A **concurrent resolution** also lacks the force of law and deals with matters in which the House and Senate must act jointly. A **joint resolution** does have the force of law and deals with unusual or temporary matters. A bill or resolution usually deals with only one topic, but a **rider** regarding an unrelated matter may be included. A rider is a proposal with little chance of passing on its own, so it is attached to a bill that probably will pass.

After a bill is introduced, it is read; the Speaker then sends it to the appropriate standing committee. Most work on bills is done in **subcommittees,** or small groups within committees. The committee may then act on the bill or set it aside and ignore it. In the latter case, a **discharge petition,** approved by a House majority, may send a bill to the floor for debate.

Once out of committee, a bill is placed on a calendar, or schedule for debating bills. Before the bill is debated, the Rules Committee must approve it or it dies.

Once on the floor, the bill is read again. In the interest of speed, the entire House may debate it as a **Committee of the Whole**—one large committee that has less strict rules than does the House. For example, the **quorum,** the number of members required to do business, is smaller for a Committee of the Whole than for the House.

Finally, a vote takes place. If approved, the bill is **engrossed,** or printed in final form. It is read once more and if approved is sent to the Senate.

THE **BIG** IDEA

A bill must move through reviews and committee hearings before it reaches the House floor; if passed, it moves to the Senate.

◼ GRAPHIC SUMMARY: *Possible Committee Actions on a Bill*

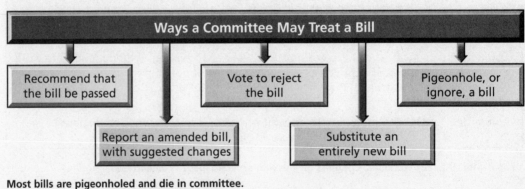

Most bills are pigeonholed and die in committee.

◼ REVIEW QUESTIONS

1. Why are some bills debated by a Committee of the Whole?

2. **Diagram Skills** How may a committee prevent a bill from advancing to the House for debate?

THE BILL IN THE SENATE

■ TEXT SUMMARY

In the Senate, a bill follows the same steps that it does in the House. However, most Senate procedures are less formal than those of the House.

Unlike the House, the Senate allows debate on bills to go on until all senators agree to end it. If one senator does not agree, debate continues and may result in a **filibuster,** a process in which a senator delays Senate action by talking at great length. The Senate can stop a filibuster only if three-fifths of the senators vote for **cloture,** or limiting debate.

For Congress to send a bill to the President, both houses must have passed identical versions of it. If necessary, a conference committee works out a compromise version that both houses will approve.

The President has ten days to act on a bill. He may sign the bill, making it a law. He may **veto,** or refuse to sign, the bill and send it back to Congress. The bill then dies unless both houses approve it again by a two-thirds vote. The President may also allow the bill to become law without a signature by not acting on it within the ten-day period. As a variation on this option, if Congress adjourns before the end of the ten-day period and the President has not signed the bill, the bill dies, a possibility called the **pocket veto.**

THE **BIG** IDEA

Although the law-making process in the Senate is much like that in the House, debate in the Senate is largely unrestricted.

■ GRAPHIC SUMMARY:
How a Bill Becomes a Law

A bill is introduced into either house and, once approved by both, passes on to the President.

Introduction to House or Senate

Committee action

Floor action

Approved bill to other house

Committee action

Floor action

To conference committee to resolve differences

Approved bill to President

Bill becomes law
or
Vetoed bill returns to Congress

■ REVIEW QUESTIONS

1. Why might a senator want to start a filibuster?

2. Diagram Skills Where do any differences the two houses introduce into a bill get resolved?

CHAPTER 12 *Test*

◼ IDENTIFYING MAIN IDEAS

Write the letter of the correct answer in the blank provided. (10 points each)

_____ 1. The most powerful leader in the House is the

   A. Speaker of the House.
   B. floor leader.
   C. majority whip.
   D. president *pro tempore*.

_____ 2. The chairmen of congressional committees are chosen by

   A. the vote of committee members.
   B. seniority.
   C. the vote of the majority party.
   D. the Speaker of the House.

_____ 3. The president of the Senate is

   A. the senator with the most seniority.
   B. the choice of the majority party caucus.
   C. the Vice President.
   D. a leading member of the majority party.

_____ 4. Which is a joint committee?

   A. a select committee
   B. a conference committee
   C. a standing committee
   D. a Committee of the Whole

_____ 5. The major job of floor leaders is to

   A. oversee House sessions.
   B. prevent filibusters.
   C. veto bills.
   D. gather party members' votes for upcoming bills.

_____ 6. In the steps of the legislative process, the event that would happen last in the House is

   A. placement on a calendar.
   B. a rule by the House Rules Committee.
   C. referral to a subcommittee.
   D. debate on the floor.

_____ 7. Which of the following has the force of law although it does not become a law?

   A. a joint resolution
   B. a bill
   C. a concurrent resolution
   D. a resolution

_____ 8. The purpose of deciding important bills by a Committee of the Whole is to

   A. ensure that every member of the House has a chance to speak about the bill.
   B. talk the bill to death.
   C. speed up the floor debate.
   D. make sure that both houses pass the same version of the bill.

_____ 9. In the steps of the legislative process, the event that would happen first is

   A. a pocket veto.
   B. placement on a calendar.
   C. a subcommittee hearing.
   D. a filibuster.

_____ 10. The President can pocket veto a bill only if

   A. it was produced by a conference committee.
   B. Congress's session is ending.
   C. Congress does not send it to him.
   D. it is a tax bill.

The Presidency

SECTION 1 · THE PRESIDENT'S JOB DESCRIPTION

■ TEXT SUMMARY

The Constitution grants the President six of his eight roles. The President acts as the ceremonial head of the government, or **chief of state.** As such, he stands as the representative of all the people of the nation. The President is also head of the executive branch, or **chief executive.** As **chief administrator,** he manages the Federal Government. As the nation's **chief diplomat,** the President sets the nation's foreign policy. The President directly controls all U.S. military forces as the **commander in chief.** He determines Congress's agenda in his role as **chief legislator.**

Two presidential roles are not defined by the Constitution. The President is **chief of party,** the unofficial head of his political party. The President is also **chief citizen** and, as such, is expected to work for and to represent the public interest.

To become President, a person must be born a citizen, be at least 35 years old, and have lived in the United States for at least the last 14 years. In 1951 the 22nd Amendment limited the presidency to two terms of four years each. The President receives a salary and benefits.

> ### THE **BIG** IDEA
>
> The President of the United States must perform eight different roles at the same time.

■ GRAPHIC SUMMARY: *The Roles of the President*

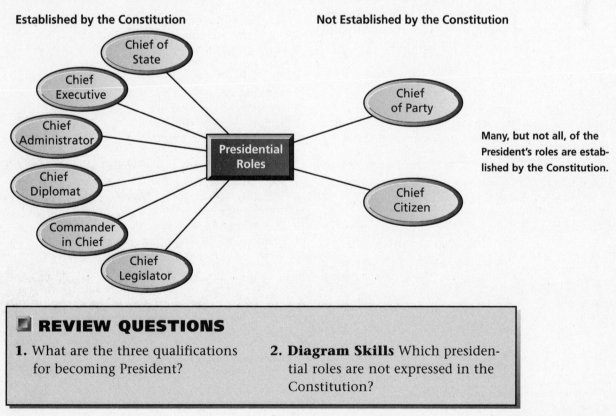

Established by the Constitution

Not Established by the Constitution

- Chief of State
- Chief Executive
- Chief Administrator
- Chief Diplomat
- Commander in Chief
- Chief Legislator

Presidential Roles

- Chief of Party
- Chief Citizen

Many, but not all, of the President's roles are established by the Constitution.

■ REVIEW QUESTIONS

1. What are the three qualifications for becoming President?

2. **Diagram Skills** Which presidential roles are not expressed in the Constitution?

PRESIDENTIAL SUCCESSION AND THE VICE PRESIDENCY

■ TEXT SUMMARY

The plan by which a vacancy in the office of President gets filled is **presidential succession.** The 25th Amendment says that the Vice President will become President if the President dies, resigns, or is removed from office. If the Vice President is unable to serve, the **Presidential Succession Act of 1947** says the Speaker of the House and the Senate's president *pro tempore* are the next officers in line.

The 25th Amendment also outlines what happens if the President becomes disabled. The Vice President becomes Acting President if the President tells Congress he cannot do his job or if the Vice President and a majority of the Cabinet tell Congress that the President is disabled.

The President may return to his duties when he thinks he is ready. If the Vice President and a majority of the Cabinet disagree, Congress must decide if the disability still exists.

Other than helping to decide about presidential disability, the Constitution assigns the Vice President only one role: presiding over the Senate. Political parties usually pick a candidate for Vice President who will **balance the ticket,** or help the presidential candidate appeal to a broader range of voters.

If the office of Vice President becomes vacant, the President chooses a replacement who must then be confirmed by a majority vote in both houses.

> ### THE **BIG** IDEA
>
> **If the President dies, resigns, or is removed from office, the Vice President succeeds to the presidency.**

There is a specific line of succession to the presidency so that the office will never be vacant.

■ GRAPHIC SUMMARY:
Presidential Succession

Order of Presidential Succession

1 Vice President
2 Speaker of the House
3 President *pro tempore* of the Senate
4 Secretary of State
5 Secretary of the Treasury
6 Secretary of Defense
7 Attorney General
8 Secretary of the Interior
9 Secretary of Agriculture
10 Secretary of Commerce
11 Secretary of Labor
12 Secretary of Health and Human Services
13 Secretary of Housing and Urban Development
14 Secretary of Transportation
15 Secretary of Energy
16 Secretary of Education
17 Secretary of Veteran Affairs
18 Secretary of Homeland Security

■ REVIEW QUESTIONS

1. Who may decide that the President is disabled?

2. Chart Skills Who becomes President if the President and Vice President are removed from office?

© Prentice-Hall, Inc.

 **SECTION 3**

PRESIDENTIAL SELECTION: THE FRAMERS' PLAN

▨ TEXT SUMMARY

The Framers debated at length about the way the President would be chosen. Most Framers opposed electing a President by Congress or by a direct vote of the people.

The Framers decided that a body of **presidential electors**, known as the **electoral college**, should choose the President and Vice President. Each of these electors cast two **electoral votes,** each one for a different candidate. The candidate with the most votes became President, and the runner-up became Vice President.

Problems with this system soon arose, partly due to the growth of political parties. In 1796 John Adams, a Federalist, was elected President. Thomas Jefferson, of the opposing Democratic-Republican party, came in second and so became Vice President.

In the election of 1800, the parties each nominated candidates for President and Vice President. Thomas Jefferson and his running mate, however, tied for electoral votes. The House of Representatives had to choose one for President; they selected Jefferson after many votes.

To avoid such problems, the 12th Amendment, passed in 1804, said electors would cast separate votes for President and Vice President. The election of 1800 also introduced the nomination of electors pledged to vote for their party's presidential ticket and the automatic casting of electoral votes in line with those pledges. Today, the President and Vice President are still formally elected by the electoral college.

> ### THE **BIG** IDEA
>
> The Framers set up an electoral college to choose the President and Vice President, but the system changed quickly.

▨ GRAPHIC SUMMARY: *The Framers' Plan for the Electoral College*

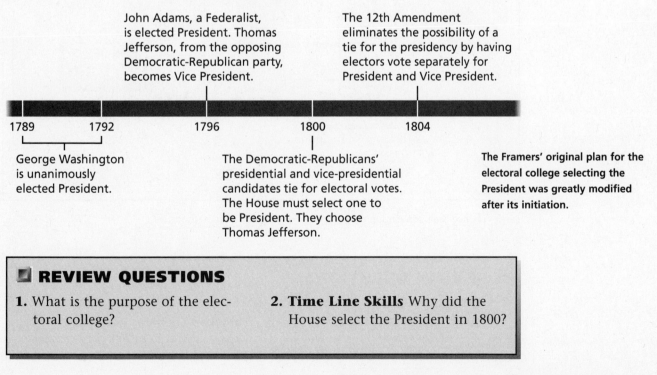

John Adams, a Federalist, is elected President. Thomas Jefferson, from the opposing Democratic-Republican party, becomes Vice President.

The 12th Amendment eliminates the possibility of a tie for the presidency by having electors vote separately for President and Vice President.

1789   1792   1796   1800   1804

George Washington is unanimously elected President.

The Democratic-Republicans' presidential and vice-presidential candidates tie for electoral votes. The House must select one to be President. They choose Thomas Jefferson.

The Framers' original plan for the electoral college selecting the President was greatly modified after its initiation.

▨ REVIEW QUESTIONS

1. What is the purpose of the electoral college?

2. Time Line Skills Why did the House select the President in 1800?

 **SECTION 4** *PRESIDENTIAL NOMINATIONS*

◼ TEXT SUMMARY

To nominate candidates for President and Vice President, each political party holds a **national convention**—a meeting at which party delegates vote. Many States use **presidential primaries,** or party elections, to help decide which delegates will go to the national conventions. The rules about primaries vary by State law. In some State primaries, voters choose convention delegates directly. In others, voters choose from among their party's candidates and the results are used to help select delegates. For the 2000 elections, primaries were held in all but six States. In non-primary States, the parties choose their candidates in local caucuses and State conventions.

A few States allow **winner-take-all** contests. That means that the winner of the primary gains the votes of all State delegates at the convention. The Democratic Party no longer allows such contests. Instead, it uses a complex system of **proportional representation** that gives each candidate that wins at least 15 percent of the primary vote a share of delegate votes.

At the national conventions, each party adopts a **platform,** or statement of its principles and objectives. The party delegates also vote for presidential and vice-presidential candidates. A stirring moment at every convention is the **keynote address,** an opening speech glorifying the party and its leaders.

> ### THE **BIG** IDEA
>
> **Every four years, political parties officially select their presidential candidates at national conventions, following State primaries and party caucuses.**

◼ GRAPHIC SUMMARY: *Selecting a Candidate for President*

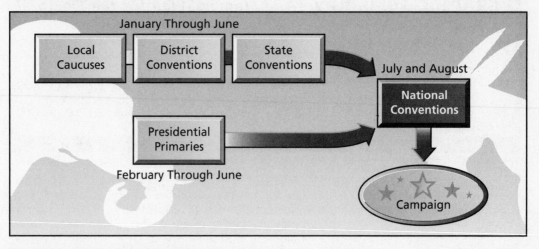

Parties choose their convention delegates by one of these two methods.

◼ REVIEW QUESTIONS

1. What is the basic purpose of a presidential primary election?

2. Diagram Skills At what four events may parties choose delegates to the national conventions?

THE ELECTION

◪ TEXT SUMMARY

The presidential campaign ends on election day, which is held every four years on the first Tuesday after the first Monday in November. Soon after, the electoral college elects the President.

When the **electorate**—the voters—vote for President, they are really voting for electors pledged to support a particular candidate. In 48 States, the candidate with the most votes from the electorate, or popular votes, wins all of the State's electoral votes. Maine and Nebraska use a district system to allot electoral votes.

Congress counts the electoral votes and declares a winner. If no candidate receives a majority of the votes, the House of Representatives elects the President.

The electoral college system has three problems. First, it is possible for the winner of the popular vote not to become President. If a candidate wins in a State by only a small majority, he still gets all its electoral votes. Also, the electoral votes are not divided according to State population and voter distribution.

Second, nothing forces a State's electors to vote for the candidate who wins the State's popular vote. Third, a strong third-party candidate could win enough votes to prevent any candidate from winning a majority, thus putting the election into the House.

Reformers have suggested four methods of changing the electoral system: the **district plan**, the **proportional plan, direct popular election**, and the **national bonus plan.** (See the Graphic Summary below.)

THE **BIG** IDEA

On election day, voters choose the next President, but the election is not official until the members of the electoral college cast their ballots.

◪ GRAPHIC SUMMARY: *Proposed Reforms to the Electoral College*

Alternative Plan	Summary of Plan
The District Plan	Electors would represent congressional districts and support the popular vote winner in their district.
The Proportional Plan	Each candidate would receive the same share of the State's electoral vote as he or she received of its popular vote.
Direct Popular Election	The voters would directly elect the President.
The National Bonus Plan	Would add to the current system by giving "bonus" electoral votes to the popular vote winner.

The proposals for changing the electoral college system have not been accepted because of much criticism against them.

◪ REVIEW QUESTIONS

1. What group officially elects the President of the United States?

2. Chart Skills Why might someone criticize the proportional plan?

CHAPTER 13 *Test*

■ IDENTIFYING MAIN IDEAS

Write the letter of the correct answer in the blank provided. (10 points each)

_____ 1. When the President determines Congress's agenda, he or she is carrying out the role of
   A. chief diplomat.
   B. chief executive.
   C. chief legislator.
   D. commander in chief.

_____ 2. In which role does the President act as a symbol of the American people?
   A. chief administrator
   B. chief of state
   C. chief diplomat
   D. chief of party

_____ 3. If the offices of both President and Vice President become vacant, who becomes President?
   A. Speaker of the House
   B. Secretary of State
   C. Secretary of Defense
   D. President *pro tempore* of the Senate

_____ 4. Who becomes Acting President if the President is disabled?
   A. the Speaker of the House
   B. the president *pro tempore* of the Senate
   C. a candidate nominated by the President
   D. the Vice President

_____ 5. When people vote for President, they are really voting for their State's
   A. primaries.
   B. caucus.
   C. electors.
   D. electorate.

_____ 6. If no candidate receives a majority of the electoral votes, the President is chosen by
   A. both houses of Congress.
   B. the House of Representatives.
   C. the Senate.
   D. a new popular vote.

_____ 7. What is the purpose of presidential primaries?
   A. to help choose delegates to the parties' national conventions
   B. to choose members of the electoral college
   C. to elect a new President and Vice President
   D. to elect State officials

_____ 8. What determines the rules for each State's primary?
   A. the Democratic Party
   B. consensus of both major political parties
   C. the Constitution
   D. State law

_____ 9. The votes of the electorate are called the
   A. electoral college vote.
   B. direct vote.
   C. popular vote.
   D. primary vote.

_____ 10. Which of the following is one criticism of the electoral college system?
   A. It underrepresents the smaller States.
   B. The winner of the popular vote might not win the presidency.
   C. It identifies the winner of the presidential election with certainty.
   D. It is unconstitutional.

The Presidency in Action

SECTION 1 — THE GROWTH OF PRESIDENTIAL POWER

◾ TEXT SUMMARY

The Constitution's **Executive Article,** Article II, gives the President some specific powers (see chart below), but it gives few details about them. Debate about the extent of these powers began with the Framers and has continued since.

Over time, the presidency has become very powerful for several reasons. First, the President stands as the executive branch's single strong leader, while Congress has two houses and over 500 members. Second, as American life has grown more complex, the people have looked to the President for leadership on such issues as the economy and health care. Third, in national emergencies, the President, as commander in chief, has needed to take decisive action. Fourth, Congress has passed many laws that expand the Federal Government's activities. Not having time itself, Congress has had to ask the executive branch to decide how to carry out these laws. Also, the President can use the **mass media**—television, radio, printed publications, and the Internet—to capture public attention.

Some past Presidents have taken a broad view of their powers, while others have said the President should have limited power. Critics of strong presidential power have used the term the **imperial presidency** to compare the President to an emperor who takes strong actions without Congress's— or the people's—approval.

THE **BIG** IDEA

The Constitution established the office of President, but debate about the extent of the office's powers has continued throughout the nation's history.

◾ GRAPHIC SUMMARY: *The Growth of Presidential Power*

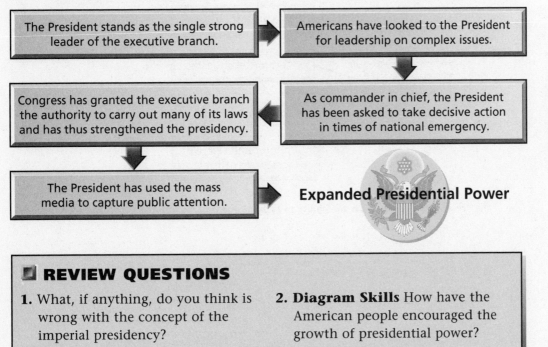

The President stands as the single strong leader of the executive branch.

Americans have looked to the President for leadership on complex issues.

Congress has granted the executive branch the authority to carry out many of its laws and has thus strengthened the presidency.

As commander in chief, the President has been asked to take decisive action in times of national emergency.

The President has used the mass media to capture public attention.

Expanded Presidential Power

Though debated, the extent of presidential power has greatly expanded due to certain factors.

◾ REVIEW QUESTIONS

1. What, if anything, do you think is wrong with the concept of the imperial presidency?

2. **Diagram Skills** How have the American people encouraged the growth of presidential power?

THE PRESIDENT'S EXECUTIVE POWERS

◾ TEXT SUMMARY

The President is the head of the executive branch and must carry out the provisions of federal law. The power to do so comes partly from the Constitution and partly from the **oath of office**—the solemn promise that each President takes at his inauguration to "preserve, protect, and defend the Constitution." The President's executive power offers him many chances to decide how laws are carried out.

The President possesses the **ordinance power,** the power to issue executive orders. An **executive order** is a directive, rule, or regulation that has the effect of law. The Constitution does not expressly give the President this power, but the President must be able to issue orders to implement his constitutional powers. Congress backs up this implied power by regularly authorizing the President to use it.

In order to have loyal subordinates, the President can choose the top officials of the executive branch, including heads of executive agencies, diplomats, Cabinet members, federal judges, and military officers. The Senate must approve these appointments with a majority vote. For State officials, the custom of senatorial courtesy holds that the Senate will approve only those appointments accepted by the State's senator from the President's party.

The President alone has the power to fire executive officials. However, the President may not remove federal judges and generally can only remove people whom he has appointed.

> ### THE **BIG** IDEA
>
> The President has great power to give orders, to decide how laws are carried out, and to appoint federal officials.

◾ GRAPHIC SUMMARY: *Major Executive Powers of the Presidency*

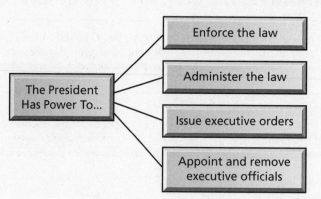

One of the President's key powers is the ability to appoint and remove top executive officials.

◾ REVIEW QUESTIONS

1. What is an executive order?

2. **Diagram Skills** How may the President affect the jobs of top executive officials?

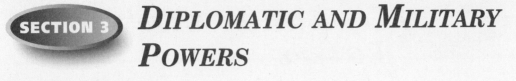

DIPLOMATIC AND MILITARY POWERS

◾ TEXT SUMMARY

The President is in charge of foreign affairs for the United States. He can make a **treaty,** or formal agreement with another nation, which must be approved by a two-thirds vote of the Senate. However, the President may avoid needing senatorial approval by making an **executive agreement,** or pact with another nation's leader.

The President also has the power of **recognition,** which is to acknowledge—and by implication support—the legal existence of another country and its government. Nations generally recognize each other by exchanging diplomatic representatives. One nation may show its strong disapproval of another by calling back its ambassador and sending the other's ambassador home. The official recalled is said to be ***persona non grata,*** or an unwelcome person.

The power to declare war belongs to Congress. However, as commander in chief, the President can still make war. More than 200 times, a President has sent U.S. forces into combat without a congressional declaration of war. After the undeclared Vietnam War, Congress passed the War Powers Resolution of 1973, designed to limit the President's war-making powers. It says that combat must stop after 60 days without the authorization of Congress.

THE **BIG** IDEA

While the President shares various diplomatic and military powers with Congress, in some areas his power is almost unlimited.

◾ GRAPHIC SUMMARY: *The Major Diplomatic and Military Powers of the President*

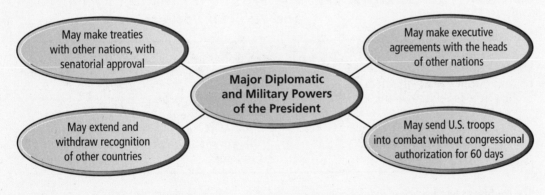

- May make treaties with other nations, with senatorial approval
- May make executive agreements with the heads of other nations
- **Major Diplomatic and Military Powers of the President**
- May extend and withdraw recognition of other countries
- May send U.S. troops into combat without congressional authorization for 60 days

The President's diplomatic and military powers give him much power to interact with other nations.

◾ REVIEW QUESTIONS

1. What does it mean when the President recognizes another country?

2. **Diagram Skills** How long may American troops stay in combat without Congress's authorization?

SECTION 4 LEGISLATIVE AND JUDICIAL POWERS

■ TEXT SUMMARY

By his legislative powers, the President may tell Congress what laws the nation needs. The President proposes some laws in an annual State of the Union address and others in an annual budget plan and economic report.

Once Congress passes a bill, the President has ten days to act on it. The President can sign the bill to make it law, allow it to become law without a signature, veto it, or use the pocket veto to let it die by not signing it before Congress adjourns. Also, from 1996 to 1998 the President had the power to use a **line-item veto** on spending and tax bills. This allowed the President to approve most of a bill while vetoing certain parts, called line items.

The Constitution also grants the President certain judicial powers. It authorizes him to grant "reprieves and pardons for offenses against the United States, except in cases of impeachment." A **reprieve** is the postponement of the execution of a sentence. A **pardon** is legal forgiveness for a crime. The pardoning power includes the powers of commutation and amnesty. **Commutation** is the power to reduce the length of a sentence or the amount of a fine imposed by a court. **Amnesty** is a general pardon offered to a group of law violators. These powers of **clemency,** that is, leniency or mercy, may only be used in cases involving federal offenses.

> ### THE **BIG** IDEA
>
> As part of the system of checks and balances, the Constitution gives the President important legislative and judicial powers.

■ GRAPHIC SUMMARY: *The President's Major Legislative and Judicial Powers*

Legislative Powers	Judicial Powers
• May recommend legislation • May veto legislation with a regular veto or with a pocket veto • May allow a bill to become a law either with or without a signature	• May grant a reprieve on a sentence • May grant a pardon for a crime • May commute the length of a sentence or the amount of a fine • May grant amnesty to a group of law violators

The President's legislative and judicial powers are part of the system of checks and balances.

■ REVIEW QUESTIONS

1. What is clemency?

2. Chart Skills How may the President veto legislation today?

CHAPTER 14 *Test*

☐ IDENTIFYING MAIN IDEAS

Write the letter of the correct answer in the blank provided. (10 points each)

____ 1. The specific powers of the President come from

    A. the military.
    B. the Supreme Court.
    C. Congress.
    D. the Constitution.

____ 2. The term *imperial presidency* refers to

    A. the use of the powers of the presidency without congressional approval.
    B. the power of the President as commander in chief.
    C. the power of the President to recognize other nations.
    D. the power of the President to impose laws on the nation.

____ 3. Which has not been a factor in the growth of presidential power?

    A. the President's ability to take military action
    B. the President's clemency powers
    C. the President's ability to use the mass media
    D. the President's position as chief executive

____ 4. What is the ordinance power of the President?

    A. the power to send U.S. troops into combat
    B. the power to issue executive orders
    C. the power to make treaties
    D. the power to pardon a person who has committed a federal crime

____ 5. The custom that gives the Senate some control over the President's power to appoint officials is called

    A. the removal power.
    B. commutation.
    C. *persona non grata.*
    D. senatorial courtesy.

____ 6. When the President recognizes a nation, he usually

    A. sends the nation a diplomatic representative.
    B. declares the nation *persona non grata.*
    C. declares war on the nation.
    D. registers strong disapproval of the nation's government.

____ 7. The length of time that a President can commit American forces to combat without the approval of Congress is

    A. 48 hours.
    B. 30 days.
    C. 60 days.
    D. 6 months.

____ 8. The President used to have the line-item veto power for which types of bills?

    A. any bills
    B. bills passed by a congressional override of a veto
    C. spending and tax bills
    D. military bills

____ 9. The presidential power of commutation allows the President to

    A. appoint officials.
    B. shorten a person's prison sentence.
    C. use the armed forces to keep the peace.
    D. veto bills.

____ 10. The President's clemency powers apply only to

    A. criminal cases.
    B. military cases.
    C. impeachments.
    D. federal cases.

Government at Work: The Bureaucracy

SECTION 1 — THE FEDERAL BUREAUCRACY

■ TEXT SUMMARY

A **bureaucracy** is a large, complex structure that handles the everyday business of an organization. It is founded on three principles. First, a bureaucracy has a hierarchical structure—a few top officials and units have authority over a large group of managers, who, in turn, supervise many more workers. Second, each **bureaucrat,** or person who works for the organization, has a specific job. Third, a bureaucracy operates under a set of formalized rules.

The federal bureaucracy is all the agencies, people, and procedures through which the Federal Government operates. The President is its chief administrator. His **administration** consists of the government's many agencies and administrators. The executive branch is composed of three groups of agencies: the Executive Office of the President, the 14 Cabinet departments, and many independent agencies.

The units of the bureaucracy go by multiple names. Departments are units of Cabinet rank. Agencies and administrations have near-Cabinet status and are each overseen by an administrator. Commissions regulate business activities and may advise on or investigate other concerns. Authorities and corporations conduct business-like activities under a board and a manager.

Each administrative organization is made up of one of two types of units. **Staff agencies** provide support for other workers, while **line agencies** perform an organization's tasks.

> ### THE **BIG** IDEA
>
> The federal bureaucracy, part of the executive branch, carries out most of the day-to-day work of the Federal Government.

■ GRAPHIC SUMMARY:
The Federal Bureaucracy

The structure of the federal bureaucracy is like a pyramid, with many more people at the bottom than at the top.

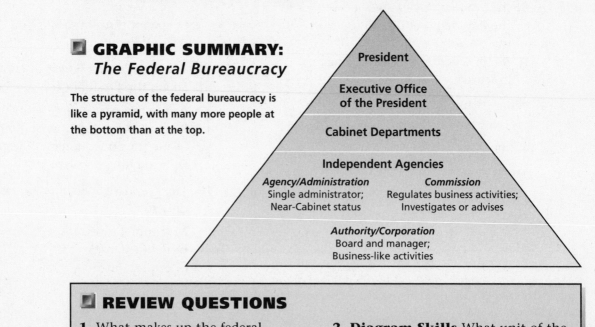

President

Executive Office of the President

Cabinet Departments

Independent Agencies

Agency/Administration
Single administrator;
Near-Cabinet status

Commission
Regulates business activities;
Investigates or advises

Authority/Corporation
Board and manager;
Business-like activities

■ REVIEW QUESTIONS

1. What makes up the federal bureaucracy?

2. **Diagram Skills** What unit of the federal bureaucracy is just below the President in rank?

THE EXECUTIVE OFFICE OF THE PRESIDENT

■ TEXT SUMMARY

The **Executive Office of the President (EOP)** is a complex organization of agencies staffed by most of the President's closest advisors and assistants.

The White House Office is the "nerve center" of the EOP. It includes the President's chief of staff, who directs White House operations, and other key members of the President's inner circle.

As part of the EOP, the National Security Council advises the President in all matters that relate to the nation's safety. The President chairs the council.

The EOP's largest unit is the Office of Management and Budget (OMB), which prepares the **federal budget.** A budget gives a detailed estimate of the money to

be received and spent by the Federal Government during the coming **fiscal year.** A fiscal year is the 12-month period used by a government or business for financial management. The Federal Government's fiscal year begins on October 1.

The EOP also includes other agencies such as the Office of National Drug Control Policy, which oversees federal efforts to fight drugs. Three of the nation's leading economists make up the Council of Economic Advisers. Still other units of the EOP deal directly with **domestic affairs,** or matters confined within the United States.

THE BIG IDEA

The Executive Office of the President includes both advisors and agencies that work closely with the President.

■ GRAPHIC SUMMARY: *The Structure of the Executive Office of the President*

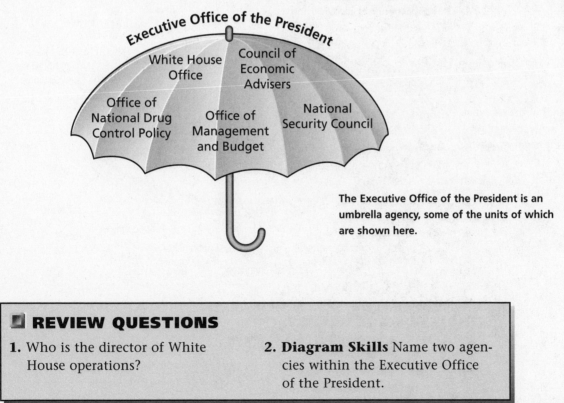

The Executive Office of the President is an umbrella agency, some of the units of which are shown here.

■ REVIEW QUESTIONS

1. Who is the director of White House operations?

2. Diagram Skills Name two agencies within the Executive Office of the President.

SECTION 3 — THE EXECUTIVE DEPARTMENTS

◪ TEXT SUMMARY

Much of the Federal Government's work is carried out by the 15 **executive departments,** the traditional units of federal administration that are often called the Cabinet departments. The Cabinet is an informal advisory board convened by the President to serve his needs; it is made up of the heads of each executive department and other top officials.

Each department head is called a **secretary,** except for the head of the Department of Justice, who is the **attorney general.** These heads act as the primary links between the President and the subunits within their departments. The President chooses each department head, but these appointments must be confirmed by the Senate.

Today, the executive departments vary in terms of visibility, importance, and size. The Department of State is the oldest and most prestigious department. The Department of Defense is the largest. The Department of Health and Human Services has the largest budget, and the Department of Homeland Security is the newest. The other departments are those of the Treasury, Justice, the Interior, Agriculture, Commerce, Labor, Housing and Urban Development, Transportation, Energy, Education, and Veterans Affairs.

> **THE BIG IDEA**
>
> Fifteen executive departments, each headed by a Cabinet member, carry out most of the Federal Government's work.

◪ GRAPHIC SUMMARY: *The Executive Departments*

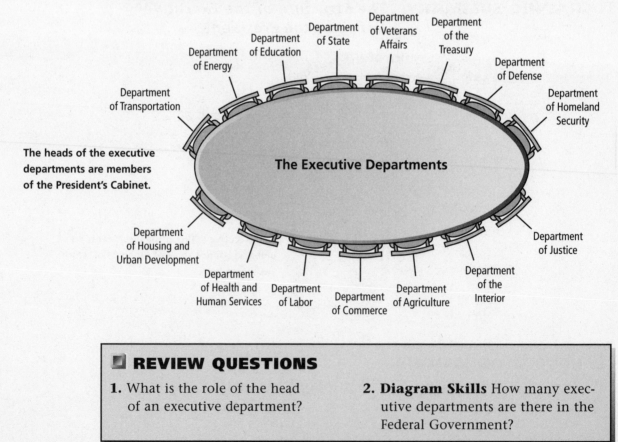

The heads of the executive departments are members of the President's Cabinet.

The Executive Departments

◪ REVIEW QUESTIONS

1. What is the role of the head of an executive department?

2. **Diagram Skills** How many executive departments are there in the Federal Government?

SECTION 4 INDEPENDENT AGENCIES

TEXT SUMMARY

Since the 1880s, Congress has created many **independent agencies,** or agencies that operate outside the executive departments. These agencies exist for a number of reasons. Some agencies do not fit well in any department. Some need protection from department politics. Others must be independent because of the nature of their functions.

Three main types of independent agencies exist today. Most are **independent executive agencies.** These are organized much like executive departments, with subunits and a single head, but do not have Cabinet status.

Independent agencies that regulate parts of the economy are **independent regulatory commissions.** Uniquely, they exist outside of presidential control, and are **quasi-legislative** and **quasi-judicial.** This means that Congress has given them certain legislative-like and judicial-like powers. Legislatively, they may make rules detailing laws that Congress has asked them to enforce; these rules carry the force of law. Judicially, they may decide disputes in the fields in which Congress has given them policing authority.

Some independent agencies are known as **government corporations.** These agencies, such as the U.S. Postal Service, carry out certain business-like activities.

THE BIG IDEA

A number of independent agencies work outside the framework of the executive branch.

GRAPHIC SUMMARY: *The Three Types of Independent Agencies*

Independent Executive Agencies	Independent Regulatory Commissions	Government Corporations
• organized like executive departments • do not have Cabinet status	• regulate parts of the economy • are quasi-legislative and quasi-judicial • exist outside of presidential control	• carry out business-like activities

There are three types of independent agencies that carry out specific duties.

REVIEW QUESTIONS

1. What defines an independent agency?

2. **Chart Skills** Which type of independent agency regulates parts of the economy?

 SECTION 5 ## THE CIVIL SERVICE

■ TEXT SUMMARY

The **civil service** is the group of public employees who perform the government's administrative work outside the military. Some of the early Presidents gave government jobs to their supporters or friends—a practice called **patronage.** The practice of giving government jobs, as well as favors, as political rewards is called the **spoils system.**

The spoils system resulted in inefficiency and corruption. Attempts to reform it began in 1881 after a disappointed office-seeker killed President James Garfield. Congress soon passed the Civil Service Act of 1883, also called the Pendleton Act, which laid the foundation for the present federal civil service system. Its main purpose was to make merit the only basis for hiring federal workers.

Today most federal employees are hired through a competitive process. They are also paid and promoted based on written evaluations from their superiors. The Office of Personnel Management, an independent agency, tests and hires most federal workers. It keeps **registers,** or lists of qualified applicants. Another independent agency, the Merit Systems Protection Board, enforces the merit principle in the federal bureaucracy. It is **bipartisan,** or made up of members from both major parties.

Civil servants must follow certain rules. Several laws and regulations place restrictions on their political activities. For example, while civil servants may be active members of a political party, they may not run in elections for that party.

> ### THE **BIG** IDEA
>
> Most of the people who work for the Federal Government are members of the civil service and are hired and promoted based on their job performance.

■ GRAPHIC SUMMARY: *The Reform of the Civil Service*

Before Civil Service Legislation	After Civil Service Legislation
Government officials give jobs and favors to friends and supporters, creating an inefficient and corrupt system of government.	Government workers are hired based on examinations, and promotions are given based on merit. The competitive nature of this system allows for higher quality work.

Today, the vast majority of civil servants are hired and promoted based on their job performance, not party membership or personal relationships.

■ REVIEW QUESTIONS

1. What is the civil service?

2. Diagram Skills How are government workers hired today?

CHAPTER 15 *Test*

☐ IDENTIFYING MAIN IDEAS

Write the letter of the correct answer in the blank provided. (10 points each)

____ 1. The federal bureaucracy is

   A. all the agencies, people, and procedures through which the Federal Government operates.
   B. hierarchical in structure.
   C. headed by the President.
   D. all of the above

____ 2. Units of Cabinet rank are called

   A. agencies.
   B. departments.
   C. commissions.
   D. administrations.

____ 3. A staff agency

   A. supports other workers.
   B. runs programs.
   C. regulates businesses.
   D. does business-like work.

____ 4. The "nerve center" of the Executive Office of the President is the

   A. Office of Management and Budget.
   B. Office of National Drug Control Policy.
   C. White House Office.
   D. Council of Economic Advisers.

____ 5. The job of the National Security Council is to

   A. advise the President about foreign trade.
   B. prepare the federal budget.
   C. supervise the civil service.
   D. advise the President about the nation's safety.

____ 6. Which is the title of the head of the Justice Department?

   A. secretary
   B. chief justice
   C. attorney general
   D. chief bureaucrat

____ 7. How many Cabinet departments are there?

   A. 15
   B. 25
   C. 100
   D. 150

____ 8. Independent regulatory commissions

   A. supervise federal workers.
   B. have some legislative-like and judicial-like powers.
   C. serve federal workers.
   D. may resemble businesses.

____ 9. After President James Garfield's assassination, the government began reforms in

   A. a number of Cabinet departments.
   B. the civil service system.
   C. the Constitution.
   D. the executive branch.

____ 10. Civil servants may not

   A. vote.
   B. belong to a political party.
   C. be promoted.
   D. run in their party's elections.

Financing Government

SECTION 1 TAXES

■ TEXT SUMMARY

The Constitution gives the power to tax to Congress, but it places limits on that power. Congress must tax in accord with all parts of the Constitution. It can set taxes for public purposes only and may not tax exports. Direct taxes, except the income tax, must be apportioned according to State population. Indirect tax rates must be the same everywhere. Congress also may not tax any governmental function of a State or its local governments.

THE BIG IDEA

The Constitution gives Congress broad power to set federal taxes, which today are collected mostly as income taxes.

Americans today pay several kinds of federal taxes. The largest source of federal revenue, the income tax, is levied on each person's yearly earnings. It is a **progressive tax,** meaning the higher the income, the higher the tax rate. Each U.S. income-earner files an annual **tax return,** a form that shows the tax owed. Businesses pay corporate income taxes.

Social insurance taxes fund three programs: Old-Age, Survivors, and Disability Insurance, known as Social Security; Medicare, or health care for the elderly; and unemployment compensation. These taxes are paid as **payroll taxes,** which employers withhold from paychecks and send to the government. Social insurance taxes are **regressive taxes,** meaning the rate is the same for everyone.

Congress places an **excise tax** on the making, selling, and using of certain goods and services. An **estate tax** must be paid on the assets of a person who has died. Gifts of over $11,000 in one year are subject to a **gift tax.** A **custom duty** is a tax laid on goods brought into the United States from another country.

■ GRAPHIC SUMMARY:
The Federal Government's Income, 2004

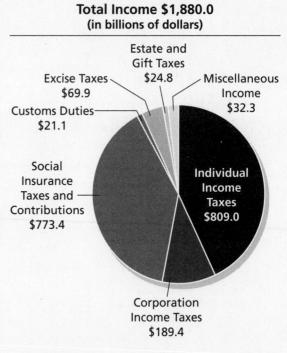

Total Income $1,880.0
(in billions of dollars)

Estate and Gift Taxes $24.8

Excise Taxes $69.9

Customs Duties $21.1

Miscellaneous Income $32.3

Social Insurance Taxes and Contributions $773.4

Individual Income Taxes $809.0

Corporation Income Taxes $189.4

The Federal Government acquires billions of dollars in revenues from taxes.

■ REVIEW QUESTIONS

1. What makes the income tax a progressive tax?

2. **Graph Skills** How much of the federal revenue came from individual income taxes in 2004?

NONTAX REVENUES AND BORROWING

■ TEXT SUMMARY

The Federal Government receives large sums of money from multiple nontax sources. Much of this money comes from the earnings of the Federal Reserve System, mostly in interest. **Interest** is a charge paid for borrowing money and is usually a percentage of the amount borrowed. Fees for such items as copyrights and trademarks also bring in money.

The Constitution gives Congress the power to authorize federal borrowing. The government borrows money at lower interest rates than do private borrowers, and there is no limit on the amount it may borrow.

These privileges allowed the Federal Government between 1929 and 1968 to regularly spend more money than it took in. This process is called running up a **deficit.** When the government takes in more than it spends, it shows a **surplus.** Since 1968, the annual federal budget has only shown a surplus between 1998 and 2001.

The annual interest on the federal debt is the amount that must be paid each year to those from whom the government has borrowed. All past deficits that are yet to be repaid, plus interest, add up to form the **public debt**—the total amount of money owed by the government. The debt has often been criticized because it causes concern for the country's future stability.

THE **BIG** IDEA

The United States has a huge public debt, created by borrowing when government spending exceeded its income.

■ GRAPHIC SUMMARY: *Budget Surplus and Deficit*

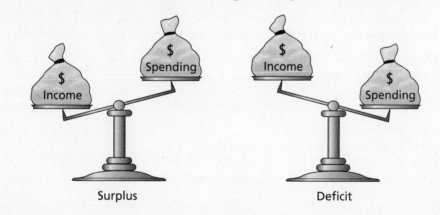

In a year when the government spends more than it takes in, it must borrow to make up the deficit.

■ REVIEW QUESTIONS

1. What is the difference between the deficit and the public debt?

2. Diagram Skills When showing a surplus, does the government take in or spend more money?

 SECTION 3 SPENDING AND THE BUDGET

TEXT SUMMARY

The largest area of government spending is for **entitlements.** These are payments made to people whom federal law says are entitled, or have a right, to them. Social Security (Old-Age, Survivors, and Disability Insurance, or OASDI) is the largest entitlement program. The next largest areas of expense are payment on the public debt and national defense.

Entitlement spending makes up part of the government's **uncontrollable spending,** that is, payments that the government is obliged by law to make each year. **Controllable spending** is spending that may be adjusted each year, such as spending on the environment or education.

The budget is the Federal Government's spending plan for one year. The President and the Office of Management and Budget put the budget together, then send it to Congress. There it goes to the Budget and Appropriations committees in each house.

The federal budget, the President's yearly plan for conducting government, is a very important document.

THE **BIG** IDEA

The annual budget-making process is a joint effort of the President and both houses of Congress.

When it has finished reviewing the budget, Congress passes a budget resolution setting spending limits for all federal agencies for the coming year. Congress then passes thirteen appropriations, or spending, bills for the year, each of which the President must sign. If all thirteen bills are not passed before October 1—the beginning of the new fiscal, or budget, year—Congress must pass a **continuing resolution.** Such a bill allows affected agencies to function until new appropriations bills are passed.

GRAPHIC SUMMARY:
Creating the Federal Budget

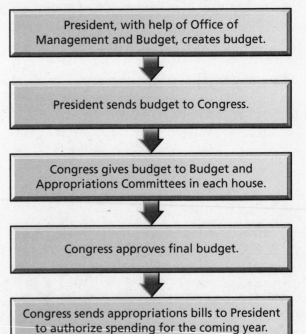

REVIEW QUESTIONS

1. How is controllable spending different from uncontrollable spending?

2. **Diagram Skills** What two branches of government prepare and approve the budget?

© Prentice-Hall, Inc.

CHAPTER 16 *Test*

■ IDENTIFYING MAIN IDEAS

Write the letter of the correct answer in the blank provided. (10 points each)

____ **1.** What part of the Federal Government has the power to tax?

   A. the President
   B. Congress
   C. the Office of Management and Budget
   D. the Treasury Department

____ **2.** A progressive tax

   A. is the same for all taxpayers.
   B. increases each year with the addition of interest.
   C. is higher in some parts of the country than in others.
   D. increases as income increases.

____ **3.** What is a tax return?

   A. a form that shows how much tax a person must pay
   B. money kept back from a worker's paycheck for taxes
   C. a tax paid by someone other than the person taxed
   D. money returned to taxpayers who paid too much in taxes

____ **4.** A custom duty is a tax on

   A. the making, selling, or using of certain products.
   B. the assets of a person who died.
   C. goods brought into the country from another country.
   D. a gift of over $10,000.

____ **5.** A deficit is

   A. the money paid for the use of a loan.
   B. the amount the government spends that exceeds its income.
   C. a plan for income and expenses.
   D. money in the federal budget that has not been spent.

____ **6.** What is the public debt?

   A. borrowed money
   B. the amount the government spends that exceeds its income
   C. the total amount of money owed by all Americans in income taxes
   D. the total amount of money owed by the Federal Government

____ **7.** Today the largest area of federal spending is for

   A. entitlements.
   B. interest on the public debt.
   C. education.
   D. national defense.

____ **8.** The Office of Management and Budget helps in the budget process by

   A. providing Congress with financial information.
   B. keeping the government running if Congress fails to pass appropriations.
   C. helping the President produce the budget.
   D. creating a budget independent of the President or Congress.

____ **9.** Another term for *appropriations* is

   A. deficit spending.
   B. spending bills.
   C. progressive taxes.
   D. entitlements.

____ **10.** A continuing resolution

   A. prepares for the next year's budget.
   B. is a measure that affects the budget year after year.
   C. allows federal agencies to function without new appropriations.
   D. is initiated in one house of Congress and carried into the other for approval.

Foreign Policy and National Defense

SECTION 1 *FOREIGN AFFAIRS AND NATIONAL SECURITY*

◼ TEXT SUMMARY

For over 150 years, Americans were more interested in **domestic affairs**—what is happening in this country—than in **foreign affairs**—events involving other countries. During that time, the United States practiced a policy of **isolationism,** or a refusal to become engaged in foreign affairs. World War II, however, convinced Americans that the well-being of the United States required their involvement in world affairs.

A nation's **foreign policy** is every aspect of its relationships with other countries—military, diplomatic, commercial, and all others. The President takes the lead in making and carrying out U.S. foreign policy.

The State Department, headed by the secretary of state, is the President's right arm in foreign affairs. International law gives all nations the **right of legation**—the right to send and receive diplomatic representatives. The President appoints **ambassadors** who each represent the nation and head an embassy in a country recognized by the United States. They and other embassy workers have **diplomatic immunity**—they cannot be prosecuted for breaking their host country's laws.

The Defense Department provides for the nation's defense by unifying the management of the armed forces. The secretary of defense is the head of the Defense Department and advises the President. The five Joint Chiefs of Staff serve as the principal military advisors to the secretary of defense. The three military departments—the Departments of the Army, the Navy, and the Air Force—are major units within the Defense Department.

THE **BIG** IDEA

Both the State Department and the Defense Department assist the President in making and carrying out foreign policy.

◼ GRAPHIC SUMMARY: *Key Players in U.S. Foreign Policy*

In the United States, the President makes and carries out foreign policy with the help of key departments.

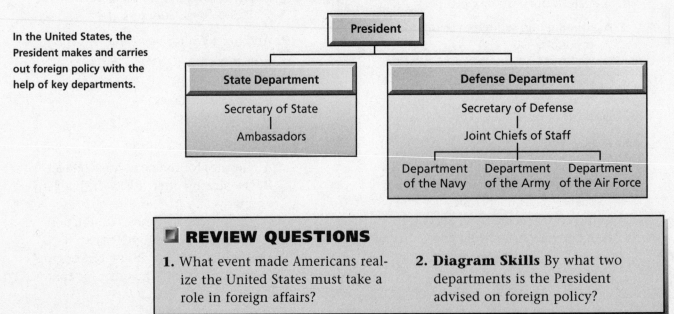

◼ REVIEW QUESTIONS

1. What event made Americans realize the United States must take a role in foreign affairs?

2. **Diagram Skills** By what two departments is the President advised on foreign policy?

OTHER FOREIGN AND DEFENSE AGENCIES

▉ TEXT SUMMARY

In addition to the Departments of State and Defense, several government agencies are closely involved with U.S. foreign and defense policy. The Central Intelligence Agency (CIA) has three major tasks. First, it coordinates the information-gathering activities of all State, Defense, and other federal agencies involved in foreign affairs and defense. Second, it analyzes that data. Third, it keeps the President and the National Security Council informed on intelligence matters. The CIA also conducts worldwide intelligence operations through **espionage,** or spying.

The Immigration and Naturalization Service (INS) enforces immigration laws and requirements. It also administers to immigrants benefits such as work permits, naturalization, and **political asylum**— safe haven for those persecuted in their home country.

The National Aeronautics and Space Administration (NASA) is an independent agency created by Congress to oversee the U.S. space programs. NASA's work ranges from exploration of outer space and the development of space stations to research on the origin and structure of the universe.

The Selective Service System manages the **draft,** or required military service. The first national draft occurred in 1917 when the Selective Service Act drafted men to fight in World War I. Between 1940 and 1973 the draft was a major source of military manpower in the United States. Although the draft ended in 1973, young men still must register for the draft soon after their 18th birthday.

THE BIG IDEA

Several government agencies are closely involved with foreign and defense policy.

▉ GRAPHIC SUMMARY: *U.S. Foreign and Defense Policy Agencies*

Agency	Function
Central Intelligence Agency (CIA)	• gathers, analyzes, and distributes intelligence information • conducts worldwide intelligence operations through espionage
Immigration and Naturalization Service (INS)	• enforces immigration laws and requirements • administers immigration benefits such as political asylum
National Aeronautics and Space Administration (NASA)	• oversees the U.S. space programs
Selective Service System	• manages the draft

Each of these federal agencies performs a function related to U.S. foreign and defense policy.

▉ REVIEW QUESTIONS

1. How is the draft implemented today?

2. Chart Skills From which federal agency could a person receive political asylum?

SECTION 3 AMERICAN FOREIGN POLICY OVERVIEW

TEXT SUMMARY

For its first 150 years, U.S. foreign policy was based on isolationism. In 1823 the Monroe Doctrine stated that the United States would keep itself out of European affairs as well as that European nations should stay out of the affairs of North and South America.

The United States was active in the Western Hemisphere, however. In the 1800s it began expanding its territory. By winning the Spanish-American War in 1898, the United States gained colonial territories and began to emerge as a world power.

In the early 1900s, the United States began forming more international relationships, such as that with China. World War II brought a final end to U.S. isolationism. Most nations at that point turned to the principle of **collective security,** by which they agreed to act together against any nation that threatened the peace. The United States also took up a policy of **deterrence**—building military strength to discourage attack. This policy began during the **cold war**—more than 40 years

of hostile relations between the United States and the Soviet Union.

During the cold war, the United States supported a policy of **containment,** which said that if communism could be contained within its existing boundaries, it would collapse under the weight of its internal weaknesses. As the United States withdrew from the Vietnam War, it began a policy of **détente**—"a relaxation of tensions"—that improved relations with the Soviet Union and China.

The end of the cold war began when Mikhail Gorbachev became the leader of the Soviet Union. U.S.-Soviet relations had improved significantly by the time the Soviet Union collapsed in 1991. Since then, some key events shaping U.S. foreign policy have occurred in the Middle East.

THE BIG IDEA

Although the United States originally followed an isolationist policy, it later became a leader in world affairs.

GRAPHIC SUMMARY: *The Changing Course of U.S. Foreign Policy*

Isolationist

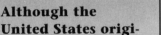

- Territorial expansion helps establish the United States as a world power.
- World War II ends isolationism and encourages a policy of collective security.
- The cold war brings about the policies of deterrence, containment, and finally détente.

World Leader

Certain events and policies have changed the United States from an isolationist nation into a leader in world events.

REVIEW QUESTIONS

1. What was the goal of deterrence?

2. **Diagram Skills** What was the effect of U.S. territorial expansion?

SECTION 4   FOREIGN AID AND DEFENSE ALLIANCES

◼ TEXT SUMMARY

For more than 50 years, a major tool of American foreign policy has been **foreign aid**—economic and military help for other nations. Foreign aid goes to countries that are the most crucial to meeting the United States' foreign policy objectives—in recent years, these have been Israel, the Philippines, and Latin American countries. Most economic foreign aid must be used to buy American goods and services, so the program also helps the U.S. economy.

Since World War II, the United States has constructed a network of **regional security alliances**—pacts in which the United States and other nations agree to work together to meet aggression in a particular part of the world. For instance, the North Atlantic Treaty Organization (NATO) promotes the collective defense of Western Europe. In areas such as the Middle East, no alliance exists because of conflicting U.S. interests—the United States has historically supported Israel while relying on Arab nations for oil.

The United States first showed its willingness to act as a world power when, after World War II, it led 50 nations in forming the United Nations (UN). The goal of the UN is world peace. It sends armed peacekeeping forces from member nations to help countries in conflict. The UN also sponsors economic and social programs, works to improve world health and protect the environment, and promotes human rights. It is composed of six major organizations: the General Assembly, the Security Council, the Economic and Social Council, the Trusteeship Council, the International Court of Justice, and the Secretariat. The **UN Security Council** bears the UN's major responsibility for maintaining international peace.

> ### THE **BIG** IDEA
>
> **The United States works with other nations to ensure peace and political stability around the world.**

◼ GRAPHIC SUMMARY: *Elements of U.S. Foreign Policy*

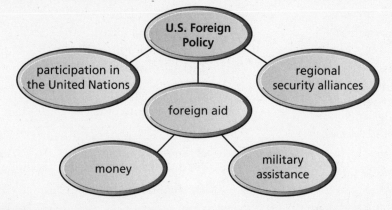

The United States' foreign policy allows it to interact with and give aid to other nations.

◼ REVIEW QUESTIONS

1. What is the purpose of a regional security alliance?

2. Diagram Skills In what forms does the U.S. provide foreign aid?

CHAPTER 17 *Test*

IDENTIFYING MAIN IDEAS

Write the letter of the correct answer in the blank provided. (10 points each)

____ 1. After World War II, the United States

   A. moved from an international role to an isolationist role.
   B. moved from security alliances to political alliances.
   C. moved from an isolationist role to an international role.
   D. formed the League of Nations.

____ 2. All are tools of U.S. foreign policy except

   A. taxation.
   B. alliances.
   C. economic and military aid to other countries.
   D. membership in the United Nations.

____ 3. Which has a key role in creating U.S. military policy?

   A. the Central Intelligence Agency
   B. the Joint Chiefs of Staff
   C. the secretary of state
   D. ambassadors and other diplomats

____ 4. All of the following play key roles in foreign policy except

   A. the National Aeronautics and Space Administration.
   B. the Selective Service System.
   C. the Department of Commerce.
   D. the Central Intelligence Agency.

____ 5. Political asylum is handled by

   A. the Selective Service.
   B. the Central Intelligence Agency.
   C. the Defense Department.
   D. the Immigration and Naturalization Service.

____ 6. The United States began to emerge as a world power after

   A. World War II.
   B. the Spanish-American War.
   C. the Revolutionary War.
   D. World War I.

____ 7. A period of détente occurred

   A. after the United States won World War II.
   B. during the early 1800s.
   C. during the early 1900s.
   D. after the United States withdrew from the Vietnam War.

____ 8. The leader who had the greatest influence on the end of the cold war is

   A. Mikhail Gorbachev.
   B. Bill Clinton.
   C. George Bush.
   D. Boris Yeltsin.

____ 9. NATO is a regional security alliance that promotes the defense of which region?

   A. Western Europe
   B. the Middle East
   C. the Philippines
   D. Latin America

____ 10. The international organization that works to maintain world peace is

   A. the League of Nations.
   B. the United Nations.
   C. the World Peace Organization.
   D. the State Department.

The Federal Court System

SECTION 1   THE NATIONAL JUDICIARY

■ TEXT SUMMARY

The Constitution creates the Supreme Court and leaves to Congress the creation of the **inferior courts**—those federal courts under the Supreme Court. Congress has created two distinct types of federal courts. Constitutional courts deal with matters involving the "judicial power of the United States." Special courts, such as the Tax Court, deal with cases related to the expressed powers of Congress.

Jurisdiction over, or the authority to hear federal cases belongs to constitutional courts. Federal courts have **exclusive jurisdiction** over cases that may *only* be heard by them. Federal and State courts have **concurrent jurisdiction** over cases that may be tried by either. Such cases may be disputes among residents of different States. In some of these cases, the **plaintiff,** the person filing the case, may choose to bring it to federal or State court. The **defendant,** the person against whom the complaint is made, may be able to have a case moved from a State court to a federal court.

A court that first hears a case has **original jurisdiction** over it. A court that hears a case on appeal from a lower court has **appellate jurisdiction** over the case.

The President nominates federal judges, and the Senate then confirms them. Judges of the Supreme Court and the constitutional courts serve for life and may only be removed from office by impeachment.

> ### THE **BIG** IDEA
>
> The Constitution outlines the structure of the federal judiciary, the jurisdiction of the courts, and the functions of federal judges.

■ GRAPHIC SUMMARY: *Types of Federal Court Jurisdiction*

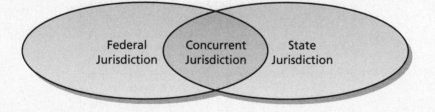

Federal Jurisdiction   Concurrent Jurisdiction   State Jurisdiction

Some cases may be tried in either a federal or a State court.

■ REVIEW QUESTIONS

1. How are federal judges appointed?

2. Diagram Skills What does *concurrent jurisdiction* mean?

 **SECTION 2** # THE INFERIOR COURTS

■ TEXT SUMMARY

The inferior courts, the federal courts under the Supreme Court, handle most federal cases. Each State, the District of Columbia, and Puerto Rico has at least one district court or federal trial court.

The 94 U.S. district courts have original jurisdiction over most federal criminal cases and federal civil cases. A federal **criminal case** is filed when a person violates a federal law. A federal **civil case** involves some noncriminal matter, such as a contract dispute.

When the Supreme Court's **docket**—its list of cases to be heard—grew too long, Congress created the courts of appeals to hear appeals from district courts. The United States now has 12 courts of appeals serving 12 judicial circuits. Altogether, 179 circuit judges sit on these appellate courts, with a justice of the Supreme Court assigned to each of them.

Congress has created two other federal courts. The U.S. Court of International Trade hears civil cases involving trade-related laws. The Court of Appeals for the Federal Circuit hears appeals cases from across the country. Its purpose is to speed up appeals in certain kinds of civil cases.

> **THE BIG IDEA**
>
> Most federal cases are tried in the inferior courts—those under the Supreme Court.

■ GRAPHIC SUMMARY: *How Federal Cases Are Appealed*

U.S. Supreme Court

12 U.S. Courts of Appeals

U.S. Court of Appeals for the Federal Circuit

94 District Courts

U.S. Court of International Trade

Congress created the courts of appeals to relieve the Supreme Court of hearing so many appeals cases.

■ REVIEW QUESTIONS

1. What defines the federal inferior courts?

2. Diagram Skills From which type of court may cases advance to the Supreme Court?

THE SUPREME COURT

▣ TEXT SUMMARY

The Supreme Court is made up of the Chief Justice and eight associate justices. It is the final authority for any case involving questions of federal law. It has the final power of judicial review, the power to decide the constitutionality of an act of government. In 1803 the Supreme Court case *Marbury* v. *Madison* established this power.

The Supreme Court has both original and appellate jurisdiction. Most of its cases come on appeal. It hears cases in original jurisdiction when either a State or a diplomat is involved.

The Supreme Court decides only about 100 cases a year. Most reach the Court by **writ of certiorari,** which is an order to a lower court to send up a case record for review. A few cases reach the Court by **certificate**—that is, a lower court asks the Supreme Court to certify an answer to a matter in its case.

When the Court accepts a case, each side sends the Court a brief—a detailed written report supporting its side of the case. Both sides then present oral arguments, after which the justices vote on the case. The justices explain their decision in writing with a **majority opinion,** which gives the Court's official position. Each of these opinions stands as a **precedent,** or an example for similar cases. A justice who agrees with the decision may write a **concurring opinion** to add points to the majority opinion. A justice who disagrees with the ruling may write a **dissenting opinion.**

> ### THE **BIG** IDEA
>
> The Supreme Court stands as the final authority on all issues pertaining to federal law.

▣ GRAPHIC SUMMARY: *How Cases Travel Through the Supreme Court*

How a Case Reaches the Supreme Court
- **by writ of certiorari:** The Supreme Court orders a lower court to send it a case's record.
- **by certificate:** A lower court asks the Supreme Court to certify a matter's answer.
- **by origination:** If a State or a diplomat is involved.

How the Supreme Court Rules on the Case
- Both sides send in briefs.
- Both sides present oral arguments.
- Justices vote and write a majority opinion.

Although most cases reach the Supreme Court on appeal, some do originate there.

▣ REVIEW QUESTIONS

1. What happens before the Supreme Court hears oral arguments?

2. Diagram Skills How does a case that reaches the Supreme Court by certificate do so?

THE SPECIAL COURTS

■ TEXT SUMMARY

The special courts of the U.S. federal court system are also called legislative courts. Each has a narrow jurisdiction, usually connected to an expressed power of Congress, such as the power to tax.

The United States cannot be sued by anyone unless Congress agrees to the case. Congress established the Court of Federal Claims to hear such cases and to allow a citizen to secure **redress,** or satisfaction of the claim, usually through payment.

Congress created territorial courts to judge cases in U.S. territories, such as the Virgin Islands. The District of Columbia, which is neither a State nor a territory, also has its own court system.

Two courts hear cases from the military. The Court of Appeals for the Armed Forces is a **civilian tribunal,** meaning that its judges are civilians. This is the court of last resort for cases involving military law. It may review the decision of a **court-martial,** or a court composed of military personnel that puts on trial those accused of violating military law.

The Court of Appeals for Veterans Claims also hears cases that involve the military. It decides appeals regarding veterans' benefits.

The Tax Court hears civil cases that involve tax law. Most of its cases are generated by the Internal Revenue Service and other agencies of the Treasury Department.

> ### THE **BIG** IDEA
>
> The special courts handle cases that are outside the mainstream judicial system.

■ GRAPHIC SUMMARY: *The Special Courts*

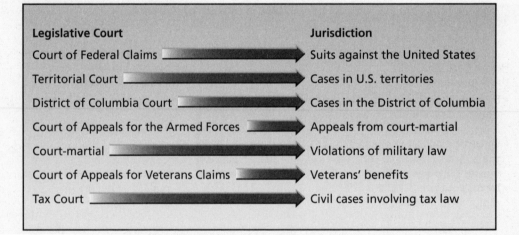

Legislative Court	Jurisdiction
Court of Federal Claims	Suits against the United States
Territorial Court	Cases in U.S. territories
District of Columbia Court	Cases in the District of Columbia
Court of Appeals for the Armed Forces	Appeals from court-martial
Court-martial	Violations of military law
Court of Appeals for Veterans Claims	Veterans' benefits
Tax Court	Civil cases involving tax law

Each special court has very narrow jurisdiction.

■ REVIEW QUESTIONS

1. On what condition may a person sue the United States?

2. Diagram Skills Which special court would hear an appeal from a court-martial?

100   **CHAPTER 18** *Guide to the Essentials*

© Prentice-Hall, Inc.

CHAPTER 18 *Test*

▉ IDENTIFYING MAIN IDEAS

Write the letter of the correct answer in the blank provided. (10 points each)

____ **1.** Who has the power to create inferior courts?

    A. the legislative courts
    B. the Supreme Court
    C. Congress
    D. the constitutional courts

____ **2.** Concurrent jurisdiction means that a case may be tried by

    A. a State court.
    B. a federal court.
    C. either a State or a federal court.
    D. the Supreme Court.

____ **3.** The plaintiff in a court case

    A. presents an oral argument before the Supreme Court.
    B. has jurisdiction over it.
    C. is the person against whom the case is made.
    D. brings the case to court.

____ **4.** The federal trial courts with original jurisdiction over most federal cases are the

    A. district courts.
    B. courts of appeals.
    C. special courts.
    D. inferior courts.

____ **5.** The United States currently has

    A. 9 federal courts of appeals, each served by a justice of the Supreme Court.
    B. 12 federal courts of appeals serving 12 judicial circuits.
    C. 179 federal courts of appeals serving 12 judicial circuits.
    D. 50 federal courts of appeals, one for each State.

____ **6.** Which court has the final power of judicial review?

    A. the Court of Federal Claims
    B. the Supreme Court
    C. the District of Columbia Court
    D. the Court of Appeals for the Federal Circuit

____ **7.** Most cases heard by the Supreme Court reach it through

    A. briefs.
    B. writs of certiorari.
    C. certificate.
    D. oral arguments.

____ **8.** A justice of the Supreme Court may write a dissenting opinion to

    A. explain why he or she disagrees with the majority opinion.
    B. add points to the majority opinion.
    C. request an appeal.
    D. establish judicial review.

____ **9.** Redress from the United States may be secured in

    A. Congress.
    B. the U.S. Court of Appeals.
    C. the Supreme Court.
    D. the Court of Federal Claims.

____ **10.** Cases from the Internal Revenue Service are often heard by the

    A. Court of Appeals for the Armed Forces.
    B. Court of Federal Claims.
    C. Tax Court.
    D. Court of Appeals for Veterans Claims.

Civil Liberties: First Amendment Freedoms

SECTION 1 · THE UNALIENABLE RIGHTS

■ TEXT SUMMARY

The Declaration of Independence states that people have certain unalienable rights, or individual freedoms that are theirs from birth. The first ten amendments to the Constitution, known as the **Bill of Rights,** list these rights.

The Constitution guarantees Americans both civil liberties and civil rights, terms that are often used interchangeably. However, **civil liberties** are protections against government acts while **civil rights** are positive acts of government that uphold the Constitution.

Each constitutional guarantee of civil liberty limits the power of government. However, Americans do not have total freedom. They may use their freedoms only in ways that do not infringe on others' rights. Most constitutional rights belong to all people living in the United States, including **aliens**—foreign-born residents or noncitizens.

The Bill of Rights applies only to the National Government. Most of its protections are applied to the State governments by the 14th Amendment's **Due Process Clause.** This clause says that "No State shall . . . deprive any person of life, liberty, or property, without due process of law." Through a series of cases, the Supreme Court has engaged in the **process of incorporation** by which most of the Bill of Rights' guarantees have been included in the Due Process Clause.

> ### THE **BIG** IDEA
>
> **Many of the Constitution's amendments guarantee the rights of the individual against the power of government.**

■ GRAPHIC SUMMARY: *The American Guarantee of Freedom*

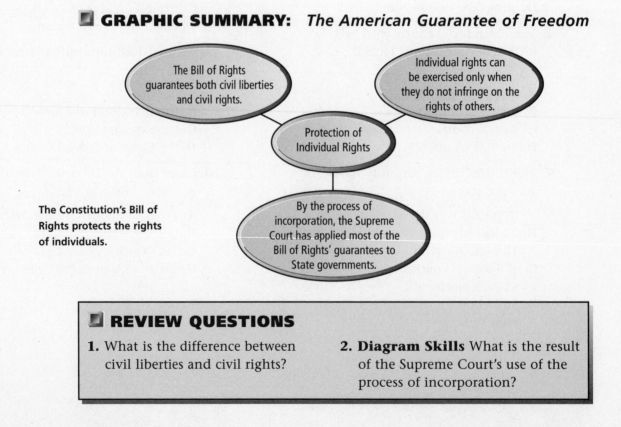

The Bill of Rights guarantees both civil liberties and civil rights.

Individual rights can be exercised only when they do not infringe on the rights of others.

Protection of Individual Rights

By the process of incorporation, the Supreme Court has applied most of the Bill of Rights' guarantees to State governments.

The Constitution's Bill of Rights protects the rights of individuals.

■ REVIEW QUESTIONS

1. What is the difference between civil liberties and civil rights?

2. **Diagram Skills** What is the result of the Supreme Court's use of the process of incorporation?

SECTION 2 | *FREEDOM OF RELIGION*

◼ TEXT SUMMARY

Free expression, including freedom of religion and freedom of the press, is necessary in a free society. The 1st Amendment guarantees religious freedom through its Establishment Clause and its Free Exercise Clause. The 14th Amendment's Due Process Clause protects this freedom from acts of the States.

The **Establishment Clause** says that "Congress shall make no law respecting an establishment of religion . . . ." Thomas Jefferson described the clause as setting up "a wall of separation between church and state." The nature of the "wall," particularly as it applies to education, is not agreed upon and has therefore been the subject of many court cases. For example, in 1925 the Supreme Court ruled that a State government could not force parents to send their children to public schools instead of private, church-related **parochial** schools.

In other rulings, the Court has said that public schools may not sponsor religious events. It has not said, however, that individuals may not pray when and as they choose—in schools or in any other place.

The **Free Exercise Clause** says that "Congress shall make no law . . . prohibiting the free exercise [of religion] . . . ." It guarantees to each person the right to believe whatever he or she wishes with regard to religion. However, no person may act on behalf of those beliefs exactly as he or she chooses. For example, people may not break laws or harm others while practicing their religion.

THE **BIG** IDEA

The Constitution's 1st Amendment guarantees religious freedom through the Establishment Clause and the Free Exercise Clause.

◼ GRAPHIC SUMMARY: *Guarantees of Religious Freedom*

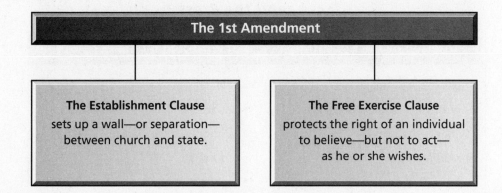

The 1st Amendment

The Establishment Clause	The Free Exercise Clause
sets up a wall—or separation— between church and state.	protects the right of an individual to believe—but not to act— as he or she wishes.

Two clauses in the 1st Amendment guarantee religious freedom in the United States.

◼ REVIEW QUESTIONS

1. What restriction is placed on the freedom of religion?

2. **Diagram Skills** Which 1st Amendment clause sets up the separation of church and state?

 # FREEDOM OF SPEECH AND PRESS

■ TEXT SUMMARY

The 1st and 14th amendments' guarantees of free speech and a free press protect a person's right to speak freely and to hear what others have to say. However, no person has the right to libel or slander another. **Libel** is the false and malicious use of printed words; **slander** is the false and malicious use of spoken words.

Sedition is the crime of attempting to overthrow or disrupt the government by force or violent acts. **Seditious speech,** or the urging of such conduct, is *not* protected by the First Amendment. The Supreme Court has limited both seditious speech and obscenity, but it seldom allows the use of **prior restraint**—the curbing by the government of ideas *before* they have been expressed.

The media are also subject to federal regulation. For instance, reporters do not have a constitutional right to keep their sources confidential. However, 30 States have passed **shield laws,** which give reporters some protection against having to disclose their sources or reveal other confidential information in legal proceedings in those States. The media of radio and television are subject to more regulation than newspapers because they use the publicly owned airwaves to distribute their materials.

Symbolic speech, or communicating ideas by conduct, has been protected by the Supreme Court. When it is peaceful, **picketing,** or the patrolling of a business site by striking workers, is one such form of protected conduct.

THE **BIG** IDEA

While the 1st and 14th amendments give Americans the right to express ideas freely, the Constitution and the Supreme Court have put some limits on free speech.

■ GRAPHIC SUMMARY: *The Rights of Freedom of Speech and the Press*

Protected by the Constitution	Not Protected by the Constitution
• right to speak freely	• libel
• right to hear what others have to say	• slander
• symbolic speech	• seditious speech
• picketing	• obscenity
	• reporters' sources

The Supreme Court both protects and limits the rights of freedom of speech and the press.

■ REVIEW QUESTIONS

1. What could the government do if it were allowed to exercise prior restraint?

2. **Chart Skills** What forms of speech are not protected by the Constitution?

SECTION 4

FREEDOM OF ASSEMBLY AND PETITION

▨ TEXT SUMMARY

The 1st and 14th amendments guarantee the right of Americans to **assemble,** or gather, to share their opinions on public matters. The people may organize to influence public policy and to tell public officials what they think. They may do this through petitions, advertisements, letters, and demonstrations. Demonstrations, however, must be peaceful. People do not have the right to block streets or close schools. They may not endanger life, property, or public order.

The government may make rules about the time and place of assemblies and about how they are conducted. These rules must be reasonable and **content neutral**—that is, the rules may not be related to what might be said at the demonstrations.

Most demonstrations take place on public property because demonstrators want to get the public's attention. There is no constitutional right to demonstrate on private property—therefore no one has a constitutional right to hand out political material or ask people to sign petitions there. Some State constitutions, however, do grant that right.

The guarantees of freedom of assembly and petition include a **guarantee of association.** That means that the right to be with others to promote political, economic, and social causes is guaranteed.

> ### THE **BIG** IDEA
>
> **The Constitution protects—but limits—the rights of Americans to gather peacefully to express their views and to petition the government.**

▨ GRAPHIC SUMMARY: *The Guarantees and Limits of Freedom of Assembly and Petition*

Guarantees	Limits
The Constitution guarantees the right to assemble peacefully and to petition the government.	While assembling, people may not endanger life, property, or public order.
Government may not make rules restricting what is said at assemblies.	Government may make rules on the time, place, and manner of assemblies.
The guarantees of freedom of petition and assembly include a guarantee of association.	The Constitution does not give the right to assemble on private property.

The Constitution protects peaceful assembly and petition but places limits on the conduct of such events.

▨ REVIEW QUESTIONS

1. What does it mean to assemble peacefully?

2. Chart Skills What is the U.S. Constitution's stance on people assembling on private property?

© Prentice-Hall, Inc.

Guide to the Essentials **CHAPTER 19** **105**

Name _____ Class _____ Date _____

Test

■ IDENTIFYING MAIN IDEAS

Write the letter of the correct answer in the blank provided. (10 points each)

_____ 1. Which of the following is guaranteed by the 1st Amendment?

    A. freedom from search and seizure
    B. freedom of religious action
    C. freedom of assembly
    D. freedom of seditious speech

_____ 2. Civil liberties are best defined as

    A. protections against government acts.
    B. positive acts of government that uphold the Constitution.
    C. all acts of government.
    D. the freedoms guaranteed to all people.

_____ 3. Aliens are

    A. people who do not live in the United States.
    B. citizens who live outside the country.
    C. noncitizens who were foreign-born.
    D. citizens who live in the United States illegally.

_____ 4. Which extends the protections of the Bill of Rights to the States?

    A. 19th Amendment
    B. 14th Amendment
    C. 5th Amendment
    D. 1st Amendment

_____ 5. Which 1st Amendment clause sets up a wall separating church and state?

    A. Free Exercise Clause
    B. Due Process Clause
    C. Necessary and Proper Clause
    D. Establishment Clause

_____ 6. Which of the following has been protected by the Supreme Court?

    A. picketing
    B. seditious speech
    C. libel
    D. slander

_____ 7. Which is an example of symbolic speech?

    A. writing something false and malicious
    B. wearing a black armband to protest war
    C. saying something false and malicious
    D. urging someone to overthrow the government

_____ 8. The Supreme Court prevents the government from using which of the following methods to control free speech?

    A. passing laws against slander
    B. hearing court cases about obscenity
    C. punishing those found guilty of libel
    D. punishing those it suspects will commit libel

_____ 9. States have given reporters some ability to protect their sources through

    A. shield laws.
    B. the Due Process Clause.
    C. freedom of association.
    D. the Establishment Clause.

_____ 10. When the government makes rules about demonstrations, the rules

    A. must not be related to the subject of the demonstration.
    B. must protect people from hearing unpleasant things.
    C. must protect public officials from criticism.
    D. must stop the demonstration from getting too large.

Civil Liberties: Protecting Individual Rights

SECTION 1 DUE PROCESS OF LAW

🔲 TEXT SUMMARY

The 5th Amendment says that the government cannot deprive a person of "life, liberty, or property, without due process of law." The 14th Amendment extends this restriction to the States. **Due process** means the government must act fairly and in accord with established rules—it must use fair procedures. Fair procedures, however, mean little if used to administer unfair laws. **Procedural due process** refers to the fair methods government must use; **substantive due process** refers to the fair policies under which government must operate.

The States have the power to protect and promote the public health, safety, morals, and general well-being of all the people. This power is called the **police power,** and the States may not use it in violation of due process. When its use conflicts with civil rights protections, the courts must balance the needs of society against individual rights. In a key case of this type, the Supreme Court supported a police officer who ordered a blood test for a suspected drunk driver even though the officer had no **search warrant,** or court order authorizing a search.

The constitutional guarantees of due process create "the right to be free . . . from unwanted governmental intrusions into one's privacy." The most controversial applications of this right have come in abortion cases.

THE **BIG** IDEA

In observing due process of law, the government must act fairly and in accord with established rules.

🔲 GRAPHIC SUMMARY: *Due Process*

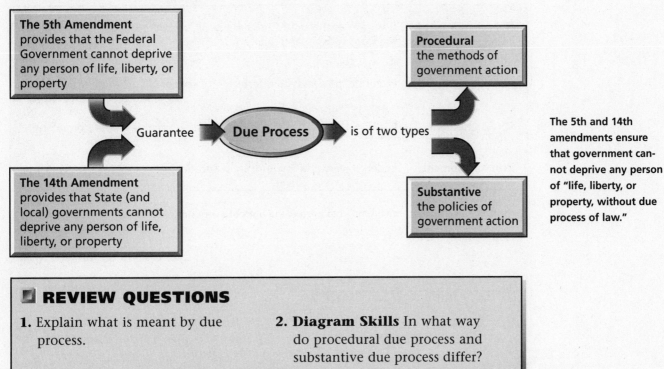

The 5th Amendment provides that the Federal Government cannot deprive any person of life, liberty, or property

The 14th Amendment provides that State (and local) governments cannot deprive any person of life, liberty, or property

Guarantee → Due Process → is of two types

Procedural the methods of government action

Substantive the policies of government action

The 5th and 14th amendments ensure that government cannot deprive any person of "life, liberty, or property, without due process of law."

🔲 REVIEW QUESTIONS

1. Explain what is meant by due process.

2. **Diagram Skills** In what way do procedural due process and substantive due process differ?

 SECTION 2

FREEDOM AND SECURITY OF THE PERSON

■ TEXT SUMMARY

The 13th Amendment was added to the Constitution in 1865 to end slavery and **involuntary servitude,** or forced labor. It covers the conduct of individuals as well as government. The Supreme Court has ruled that the 13th Amendment authorizes Congress to attack racial **discrimination,** that is, bias or unfairness.

The 2nd Amendment protects the right of each State to keep a militia. It does not guarantee the right of individuals to keep and bear arms. The Supreme Court has never found that right to be within the 14th Amendment's Due Process Clause. Each State can therefore create its own limits on the right to keep and bear arms—and all of the States do, in various ways.

The 3rd and 4th amendments guarantee that government cannot disturb people or their homes without good reason. The 3rd Amendment forbids the unlawful quartering of soldiers in private homes—a British practice in colonial days. The 4th Amendment also grew out of colonial practice. It requires that, to search for or seize evidence or persons, police officers have a proper warrant obtained with **probable cause**—a reasonable suspicion of crime. It was designed to protect against the colonial use of **writs of assistance**—blanket search warrants that allowed British officers to search private homes. The **exclusionary rule** says that evidence gained by illegal police action, such as searching without a warrant, cannot be used against the person from whom it was seized.

> ### THE **BIG** IDEA
>
> Several of the Constitution's provisions protect the rights of people to be free from physical restraints and to be secure in their persons and homes.

■ GRAPHIC SUMMARY: *The Security Amendments*

2nd Amendment	Gives States the right to maintain militias; does not give individuals the right to keep and bear arms
3rd Amendment	Prohibits the unlawful quartering of soldiers in private homes
4th Amendment	Prevents unlawful searches and seizing of people or their property
13th Amendment	Ended slavery and involuntary servitude

The security amendments are intended to protect the right of every American to live in freedom.

■ REVIEW QUESTIONS

1. Why was the 2nd Amendment added to the Constitution?

2. **Chart Skills** Which amendment prevents police from searching a house without a warrant?

RIGHTS OF THE ACCUSED

▣ TEXT SUMMARY

The Constitution offers several guarantees for persons accused of crimes. For one, it grants the right to seek a **writ of habeas corpus**—a court order commanding an officer imprisoning someone to explain why the prisoner should not be released. It also prohibits the passage of a **bill of attainder,** which punishes a person without a trial. Also, Congress and the States may not pass an **ex post facto law,** which makes an act a crime and then punishes someone for committing the act before the law's passage.

A **grand jury** decides if someone can be accused of a serious crime. The prosecutor presents the grand jury with an **indictment,** or a formal complaint against the accused. The grand jury decides whether there is enough evidence for a trial; if not, the charges are dropped. In most States today a prosecutor brings charges in an information—a document in which he or she swears there is enough evidence for a trial.

An accused person may not be exposed to **double jeopardy,** that is, be tried for the same crime more than once. The person has the right to a speedy and public trial by jury with the assistance of counsel (a lawyer). If a defendant waives this right, a **bench trial** is held, meaning a judge alone hears the case.

The 5th Amendment protects a person from self-incrimination, or being a witness against himself or herself. The **Miranda Rule** requires police to read a list of rights to a person they arrest and make sure the person understands these rights.

▣ GRAPHIC SUMMARY:
Constitutional Protections for Persons Accused of Crimes

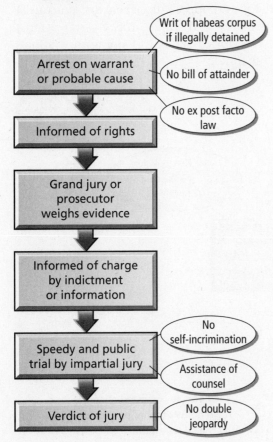

THE BIG IDEA

The American judicial system presumes that any person accused of a crime is innocent until proven guilty, and the Constitution upholds the rights of the accused.

The Constitution ensures that a person accused of a crime is presumed innocent until proven guilty.

▣ REVIEW QUESTIONS

1. What is the effect of a writ of habeas corpus?

2. **Diagram Skills** What are two protections given by a speedy and public trial by jury?

PUNISHMENT

■ TEXT SUMMARY

The 8th Amendment offers protections for Americans being punished for crimes. It forbids the setting of excessive or unreasonably high bail. **Bail** is a sum of money that an accused person must pay the court as a guarantee that he or she will appear in court at the proper time. Once paid, the person goes free until the time of the trial. If the defendant does not come to court, he or she does not get the money back.

In 1984 Congress provided for the **preventive detention** of some people accused of committing federal crimes. This means that federal judges may keep accused felons in jail without bail when there is reason to believe that they will commit additional crimes before trial.

The 8th Amendment also forbids cruel and unusual punishment, such as burning at the stake or crucifixion. The Supreme Court has held that **capital punishment,** or the death penalty, is constitutional if applied fairly.

Treason is the only crime the Framers specifically defined in the Constitution; they wanted to prevent tyrants from using the charge of treason to punish political opponents. **Treason** can consist of only two things: making war against the United States and aiding the nation's enemies.

> ### THE **BIG** IDEA
>
> In addressing the issue of punishment for crime, the 8th Amendment forbids excessive bail and cruel and unusual punishment.

■ GRAPHIC SUMMARY:
Protections in Punishment of Crimes

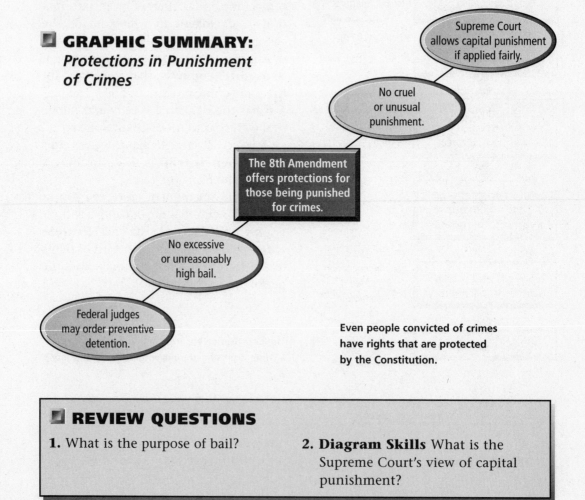

Even people convicted of crimes have rights that are protected by the Constitution.

■ REVIEW QUESTIONS

1. What is the purpose of bail?

2. Diagram Skills What is the Supreme Court's view of capital punishment?

CHAPTER 20 *Test*

◼ IDENTIFYING MAIN IDEAS

Write the letter of the correct answer in the blank provided. (10 points each)

____ 1. Which amendment says the government must follow due process of law before punishing a person for committing a crime?

   A. 1st Amendment
   B. 5th Amendment
   C. 8th Amendment
   D. 14th Amendment

____ 2. The requirement that government operate under fair policies is called

   A. procedural due process.
   B. involuntary servitude.
   C. substantive due process.
   D. the exclusionary rule.

____ 3. Before police officers search a house for evidence, they must have

   A. a search warrant.
   B. a writ of habeas corpus.
   C. police power.
   D. a bill of attainder.

____ 4. The 2nd Amendment states that

   A. each State may keep a militia.
   B. each American is entitled to possess a weapon.
   C. people accused of crimes do not have to incriminate themselves.
   D. involuntary servitude is unconstitutional.

____ 5. Evidence gained by the police from an illegal act is subject to which rule?

   A. ex post facto law
   B. the exclusionary rule
   C. probable cause
   D. the Miranda Rule

____ 6. A person is stopped by police and held in jail for several days without a hearing. Which of the following should the person seek?

   A. a bill of attainder
   B. an ex post facto law
   C. a writ of habeas corpus
   D. an indictment

____ 7. The decision of whether a person can be accused of a serious crime is made by

   A. a prosecutor.
   B. counsel.
   C. a grand jury.
   D. a bench trial.

____ 8. Trying a person for the same crime more than once is called

   A. capital punishment.
   B. presentment.
   C. bills of attainder.
   D. double jeopardy.

____ 9. Which allows federal judges to keep accused felons in jail without bail?

   A. the 8th Amendment
   B. the Miranda Rule
   C. writs of assistance
   D. preventive detention

____ 10. The only crime specifically defined by the Framers of the Constitution is

   A. capital punishment.
   B. treason.
   C. discrimination.
   D. presentment.

Civil Rights: Equal Justice Under Law

SECTION 1 — DIVERSITY AND DISCRIMINATION IN AMERICAN SOCIETY

▉ TEXT SUMMARY

The United States is a **heterogeneous** society—it is composed of people from different backgrounds. Since the 1960s, the ethnic makeup of the country has changed. Near-record numbers of **immigrants,** or people legally admitted as permanent residents, have helped increase the numbers of African, Asian, and Hispanic Americans. Many recent Hispanic immigrants have come from Central and South America as **refugees,** or people who leave their homes to seek protection from danger.

Assimilation is the process by which people of one culture merge into and become part of another culture. In our history, white Americans have not been very good at giving an equal place to nonwhite Americans.

African, Native, Hispanic, and Asian Americans are four large minority groups that have suffered discrimination from the government and private individuals. Today, more than one-third of the nation's Native American population lives on **reservations**—public lands set aside for use by Native American tribes.

Women experience discrimination in much the same way that minorities do. They have been treated as less than equal in property rights, education, and employment opportunities.

> **THE BIG IDEA**
>
> **While the United States has struggled to meet the constitutional ideal of equality for all, members of ethnic minorities and women have faced discrimination.**

▉ GRAPHIC SUMMARY: *Heterogeneous American Society*

Heterogeneous Society:	*A society made up of people from different backgrounds* The United States is a heterogeneous society, composed of whites, Native Americans, and many other ethnic groups.
Immigrants:	*People legally admitted to a country as permanent residents* Many African, Asian, and Hispanic immigrants reside in the United States.
Refugees:	*People who leave their homes to seek protection from war, persecution, or some other danger* Many refugees from Central and South America reside in the United States.
Assimilation:	*The process by which people of one culture merge into and become part of another culture* The white population in the United States has tried to assimilate all nonwhite groups into it.
Discrimination:	*The mistreatment of one group of people by another* Ethnic minorities and women face discrimination in the United States.

Although the United States is home to people of many backgrounds, women and ethnic minorities have experienced discrimination.

▉ REVIEW QUESTIONS

1. In what ways have women been discriminated against in the United States?

2. **Chart Skills** What defines a heterogeneous society?

EQUALITY BEFORE THE LAW

■ TEXT SUMMARY

Government needs the power to discriminate, or treat groups differently. For example, it may treat minors differently than it does adults. However, this power must be limited so that there is equal protection under the law for all Americans.

Segregation is the separation of one group from another. In 1868 the 14th Amendment guaranteed equal protection under the law to all Americans. However, States quickly passed **Jim Crow laws** that segregated African Americans, meaning they could not share facilities with whites. In 1896 the Supreme Court gave these laws constitutional support with the **separate-but-equal doctrine.** In *Plessy* v. *Ferguson,* it ruled that separate facilities of supposed equal quality for whites and African Americans were constitutional.

However, the Supreme Court has since overturned many of the Jim Crow laws. In 1954 *Brown* v. *Board of Education of Topeka* struck down the separate-but-equal ruling. Then the country made a start toward **integration**—the process of bringing a group into equal membership in society. The Civil Rights Act of 1964 forbade the federal funding of State or local activities that support racial segregation. Finally, in 1970 **de jure segregation**—legally sanctioned segregation—in schools was abolished. However, many communities still have **de facto segregation**—segregation in fact, even if no law requires it—which is often caused by housing patterns.

Gender has long been another basis for unequal treatment. However, since 1971 courts have successfully challenged most laws that allow different treatment of men and women.

THE **BIG** IDEA

Federal law now includes safeguards to protect Americans from discrimination on the basis of race or sex.

■ GRAPHIC SUMMARY:
The Path to Equality Before the Law

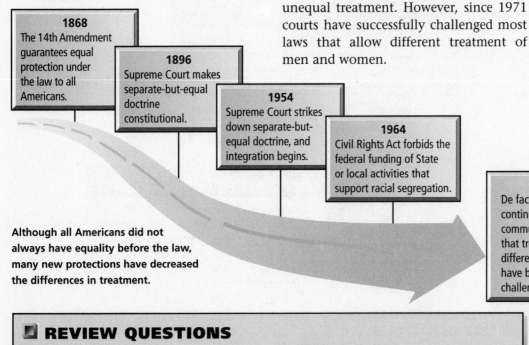

1868
The 14th Amendment guarantees equal protection under the law to all Americans.

1896
Supreme Court makes separate-but-equal doctrine constitutional.

1954
Supreme Court strikes down separate-but-equal doctrine, and integration begins.

1964
Civil Rights Act forbids the federal funding of State or local activities that support racial segregation.

Present
De facto segregation continues in many communities. Most laws that treat women differently from men have been successfully challenged in court.

Although all Americans did not always have equality before the law, many new protections have decreased the differences in treatment.

■ REVIEW QUESTIONS

1. What is integration?

2. Diagram Skills What constitutional amendment guarantees equal treatment under the law?

FEDERAL CIVIL RIGHTS LAWS

◼ TEXT SUMMARY

From the 1870s to the late 1950s, Congress passed no civil rights legislation. Since then, much has been passed. One of the strongest was the Civil Rights Act of 1964. It says that everyone, regardless of race, color, religion, or national origin, is free to use "public accommodations" such as hotels and restaurants. It also prohibits discrimination—in the workplace and in any program receiving federal funding—based on the reasons above or physical disability, age, or gender. The Civil Rights Act of 1968 prohibits discrimination in the selling or leasing of housing.

In the 1960s, the Federal Government also began **affirmative action**—a policy requiring employers to take positive steps to remedy the effects of past discrimination. An employer must make its work force reflect the general makeup of the population in its locale and correct inequalities in pay, promotions, and benefits. Rules that call for certain numbers of jobs or promotions to be kept for certain groups are called **quotas.** Affirmative action applies to all government offices and all businesses that work with the government.

Affirmative action has been criticized for being **reverse discrimination,** or discrimination against the majority group. Supporters and critics of the policy have taken their arguments to the Supreme Court, State legislatures, and the voting booth, where the debate continues.

> ### THE **BIG** IDEA
>
> Federal laws passed in the 1950s and 1960s began the challenge against long-standing discrimination.

◼ GRAPHIC SUMMARY: *Key Federal Civil Rights Laws*

Civil Rights Act of 1964

Prohibits discrimination in public accommodations, in the workplace, and in any program receiving federal funding.

Civil Rights Act of 1968

Prohibits discrimination in the selling or leasing of housing.

Affirmative Action

Requires employers to take positive steps to remedy the effects of past discriminations; they must adopt plans to make their work force reflect the general makeup of the population in their locale.

The civil rights movement has led to the passage of civil rights acts and affirmative action policies.

◼ REVIEW QUESTIONS

1. What is the purpose of affirmative action?

2. **Chart Skills** What law forbids housing discrimination?

AMERICAN CITIZENSHIP

TEXT SUMMARY

The vast majority of people living in the United States are American **citizens**—people who owe loyalty to the United States and, in turn, receive its protection. Most Americans are citizens because they were born in this country—because of **jus soli,** or the law of the soil—where one is born. Because of **jus sanguinis,** or the law of the blood—to whom one is born—a child born abroad can become an American citizen at birth if he or she is born to a parent who is a citizen and who has lived in the United States at some time.

Several million **aliens**—citizens or nationals of a foreign country who live in the United States—become citizens at some time after birth through the legal process of **naturalization,** over which Congress has exclusive control. States have no power in the matter.

Americans can choose to give up, or voluntarily abandon, their citizenship. This occurs through the legal process of **expatriation.** Naturalized citizens who have gained citizenship through fraud or deception may lose their citizenship through a court-ordered process called **denaturalization.**

Most immigrants to the United States have entered the country officially. Many others, however, arrive illegally and then face special challenges to stay in this country. Congress has the power to place and remove immigration restrictions. Aliens may be subject to **deportation,** a legal process in which they are required to leave the United States.

THE BIG IDEA

People can receive American citizenship through birth, from their parents, or through the naturalization process.

GRAPHIC SUMMARY: *Ways of Gaining and Losing American Citizenship*

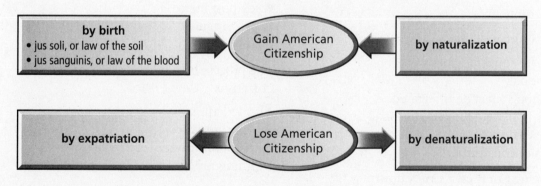

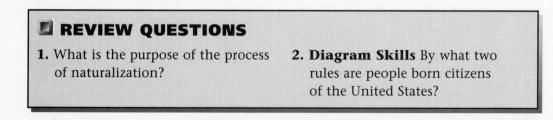

Americans must qualify for citizenship; they may also give up their citizenship or have it taken from them.

REVIEW QUESTIONS

1. What is the purpose of the process of naturalization?

2. Diagram Skills By what two rules are people born citizens of the United States?

CHAPTER 21 *Test*

◼ IDENTIFYING MAIN IDEAS

Write the letter of the correct answer in the blank provided. (10 points each)

____ 1. The United States is a heterogeneous society because

   A. most of its residents are not citizens.
   B. it is made up of people from different backgrounds.
   C. most of its residents have European ancestors.
   D. it allows few immigrants.

____ 2. Which of the following groups have suffered as part of discrimination in the United States?

   A. women
   B. African Americans and Asian Americans
   C. Native Americans and Hispanic Americans
   D. all of the above

____ 3. Which promises equal protection under the law?

   A. 1st Amendment
   B. 10th Amendment
   C. 14th Amendment
   D. 19th Amendment

____ 4. In 1896 the Supreme Court ruled that

   A. separate-but-equal facilities were constitutional.
   B. public schools must be integrated.
   C. Jim Crow laws were unconstitutional.
   D. housing discrimination could be viewed as unconstitutional.

____ 5. Which Supreme Court case struck down the separate-but-equal ruling?

   A. *Plessy* v. *Ferguson*
   B. *Brown* v. *Board of Education of Topeka*
   C. *Regents of the University of California* v. *Bakke*
   D. *Bradwell* v. *Illinois*

____ 6. Which kind of segregation is often caused by housing patterns?

   A. Jim Crow segregation
   B. de facto segregation
   C. jus sanguinis segregation
   D. de jure segregation

____ 7. The governmental policy that attempts to make up for past discrimination is

   A. expatriation.
   B. deportation.
   C. reverse discrimination.
   D. affirmative action.

____ 8. The vast majority of Americans are

   A. aliens.
   B. expatriates.
   C. citizens.
   D. immigrants.

____ 9. People born in the United States are citizens by

   A. jus soli.
   B. ex post facto.
   C. jus sanguinis.
   D. de jure.

____ 10. The process by which aliens become citizens is

   A. reservation.
   B. discrimination.
   C. naturalization.
   D. immigration.

Comparative Political Systems

CHAPTER 22

SECTION 1 · HISTORICAL POLITICAL SYSTEMS

■ TEXT SUMMARY

In response to the chaos in Europe after the fall of Rome, the system of **feudalism** developed. Under a feudal system, government was based on a network of personal relationships between powerful lords and their **vassals**. The lord gave land and protection to his vassals, and expected loyalty and service in return. At the bottom of this system were the **serfs**, who were bound to their land and had no say in the system.

Feudalism worked well in Europe while the economy was simple and the society's values were fairly uniform. But eventually cities grew, the economy became more complex, and the Protestant Reformation led to widespread upheaval, leading to the Thirty Years' War. Feudalism could not cope with these shocks. It became clear that Europeans needed stronger central governments and clearly defined sovereign states. Kings and queens, because of their strong position in the feudal system, were recognized as the leaders of their states.

The new central governments became even more powerful by adopting **mercantilism**, which was a policy that foreign trade ought to increase the wealth of the state. Mercantilism was important as the European states established colonies in the New World, since the colonies represented new markets for the home country's trade. Since only the state could set up new colonies, this made the state's role even more important.

> ### THE **BIG** IDEA
>
> As cities grew and trade increased, feudalism led to modern, sovereign states.

■ GRAPHIC SUMMARY: *Feudalism and Sovereignty*

Feudalism	Sovereign States
• Followed the fall of the Roman Empire	• Began with Peace of Westphalia in 1648
• Weak monarch	• Strong monarch
• Weak sense of boundaries, multiple rulers over land	• Defined boundaries for countries
• Basic economy built on labor, local goods, and barter	• Complex economy with trade, cities, and money

Sovereign states replaced the feudal system in Western Europe.

■ REVIEW QUESTIONS

1. Why did kings and queens pursue mercantilist policies?

2. Chart Skills What are the main differences between a feudal system and a sovereign government?

IDEAS AND REVOLUTIONS

■ TEXT SUMMARY

Early European monarchs claimed that their rule was legitimate because of the **divine right of kings**—they said God gave them the authority to rule. People started to Challenge this idea, and soon the principle of popular sovereignty, that the government's legitimacy comes from the people themselves, became more important.

> ### THE **BIG** IDEA
>
> **Popular sovereignty is the basis for most modern governments, including both democracies and dictatorships.**

Countries have taken many different paths towards popular sovereignty. In Britain, the government gradually changed from an absolute monarchy into a democracy. As a result change came very slowly. By contrast, in France the change came by revolution over the course of just a few years. The revolution was violent, and many old French institutions and traditions were abandoned.

In Latin America, under the **encomienda** system, power was centered on the *haciendas*, or large estates. This system made it difficult to build strong central governments when Latin American countries became independent.

In Africa, the problems faced have been even more complex. Many African countries, such as Nigeria, include multiple ethnic groups that speak many different languages and observe different religions. The problem of building stable governments in Africa is worsened by difficult economic conditions.

Communism and **fascism**, two systems in which state power is strongly centralized and people have no say in their government, caused great violence in the 20th century. These systems are very different, but they both twist the idea of popular sovereignty, claiming that the state governs in the name of the people. In fact, both systems of government are dictatorships.

■ GRAPHIC SUMMARY: *The Challenges of Independence*

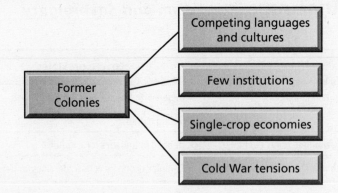

Competing languages and cultures

Few institutions

Former Colonies

Single-crop economies

Cold War tensions

Many former colonies struggled after independence.

■ REVIEW QUESTIONS

1. What arguments did communist and fascist governments use to claim that their dictatorships government on behalf of the people? How did their arguments differ?

2. **Diagram Skills** How has colonialism has made it harder to build stable governments in Africa?

TRANSITIONS TO DEMOCRACY

TEXT SUMMARY

In recent years, many countries have moved from dictatorship to democracy. This transition has taken many forms. Often the first step is an argument between **hardliners** and **softliners** as to how to handle reform within the government. Hardliners do not want reform, while softliners support reform in order to keep the government in power longer.

In Poland, in response to economic problems, Lech Walesa and the Solidarity trade union persuaded softliners within the communist government to grant them some fundamental rights. Ultimately the dictatorship fell, and Walesa became Poland's first democratically elected president. Similarly, in the former Soviet Union the transition began when Mikhail Gorbachev took soft-line, reform positions known as *glasnost* (openness) and *perestroika* (restructuring). Russian president Boris Yeltsin then demanded further reforms, and the Soviet Union collapsed.

The final step in democratization is **democratic consolidation**—building strong institutions to make sure democracy survives. Where democratic institutions are weak, the government can often return to dictatorship or fall into civil war. In some cases, the problems become so serious that the government disappears. These **failed states**, such as Somalia or Afghanistan, can provide homes for terrorists.

THE BIG IDEA

To successfully change from dictatorship to democracy, countries must build strong institutions that the people trust and respect.

GRAPHIC SUMMARY: *The Path to Russia*

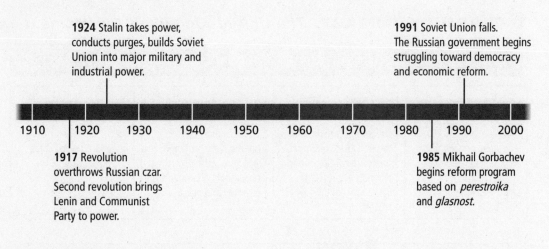

1924 Stalin takes power, conducts purges, builds Soviet Union into major military and industrial power.

1991 Soviet Union falls. The Russian government begins struggling toward democracy and economic reform.

1910 1920 1930 1940 1950 1960 1970 1980 1990 2000

1917 Revolution overthrows Russian czar. Second revolution brings Lenin and Communist Party to power.

1985 Mikhail Gorbachev begins reform program based on *perestroika* and *glasnost.*

Since the fall of the Soviet Union, Russia has begun struggling toward democracy.

REVIEW QUESTIONS

1. What factors are necessary to bring about democratic consolidation? Why is this process so difficult?

2. **Time Line Skills** At what point was Russia able to strive for democracy?

WORLD DEMOCRACIES TODAY

◪ TEXT SUMMARY

Not all democracies have the same structure. Each democratic country has created a system of government that is unique to that country's history and values.

The government of Great Britain does not have a single written constitution. Britain is also still a monarchy, although the queen has no actual power to govern. Instead, Britain is governed by its parliament, which includes the House of Lords and the House of Commons. Instead of a president, Britain has a prime minister, who is always the leader of the largest party in the House of Commons. The prime minister chooses the other **ministers** in the government from among the members of his party in Parliament. Since voting in Parliament is almost always along party lines, the Prime Minister only rarely fails to get a bill passed. When an important bill fails, the Prime Minister usually resigns and asks the monarch to call a new election of Parliament.

Mexico's government is more similar to American government. Mexico has a president, who is elected to a single six-year term. Unlike in the U.S., the president of Mexico can propose constitutional amendments and enact laws by decree. Mexico's legislature consists of a Senate and a Chamber of Deputies. Mexico's senate has two representatives from each Mexican state. Mexico, like the U.S. and unlike Britain, is a federal system; Mexico's 31 states are governed by separate state governments. For years, Mexico was governed by just one party, the PRI. PRI's monopoly on power weakened beginning in the 1980's, and was broken with the election of president Vicente Fox in 2000.

> ### THE **BIG** IDEA
>
> **Great Britain and Mexico are two examples of successful democracies that differ from American democracy in key ways.**

◪ GRAPHIC SUMMARY: *The United Kingdom's Government*

Although the UK is a monarchy, the real exercise of governmental power is by the prime minister and Parliament.

Aspects of the United Kingdom's Government

Unitary	Parliamentary	Constitutional	Monarchy
The executive and legislative powers of government reside in one central agency—Parliament.	Parliament is divided into the House of Lords and the House of Commons. The prime minister is selected from the House of Commons.	Government rests upon a constitution, which consists of written documents and unwritten customs and practices.	Today, the monarch is a figurehead who reigns but does not rule.

◪ REVIEW QUESTIONS

1. The structure of Mexican government is similar to America's, yet Mexico was for many years considered undemocratic. How did the PRI's rule make Mexico undemocratic?

2. Diagram Skills What are the most important differences between the governmental systems of the United States and Britain?

Name _____ Class _____ Date _____

☐ IDENTIFYING MAIN IDEAS

Write the letter of the correct answer in the blank provided. (10 points each)

____ 1. Feudalism built on relationships between lords and weaker nobles called

A. ministers.
B. vassals.
C. manors.
D. serfs.

____ 2. Mercantilism was a theory that

A. lords and vassals should rule through loose agreements.
B. kings and queens ruled by God's will.
C. money from foreign trade should enrich the state.
D. governments should not interfere with businesses.

____ 3. The idea that a government's legitimacy comes from the people is

A. popular sovereignty.
B. divine right.
C. constitutional monarchy.
D. feudalism.

____ 4. Which of the following is normally NOT a feature of a communist government?

A. it rules as a dictatorship
B. it establishes colonies all around the world
C. it claims to rule on behalf of the people
D. it controls the means of production

____ 5. People within a dictatorship who reject democratic reforms are

A. solidarity.
B. hardliners.
C. softliners.
D. *hacienda*.

____ 6. One example of a failed state is

A. Great Britain
B. Nigeria
C. Mexico
D. Somalia

____ 7. France's transition to popular sovereignty was led by

A. slow, gradual change.
B. guerrilla warfare and military coups.
C. a quick and violent revolution.
D. a foreign invasion and nation-building.

____ 8. Which of the following countries is a monarchy?

A. Britain
B. France
C. Russia
D. Mexico

____ 9. The prime minister of Britain is

A. popularly elected.
B. appointed by the House of Representatives.
C. the leader of the majority party in the House of Commons.
D. appointed by the president.

____ 10. The political party that held power in Mexico for much of the 20th century is the

A. PAN.
B. PRI.
C. NAFTA
D. CCP.

Comparative Economic Systems

SECTION 1 CAPITALISM

■ TEXT SUMMARY

In any economy, the basic resources used to make all goods and services—land, labor, and capital—are called **factors of production.** Land includes all natural resources. Labor refers to the people who do an economy's work. **Capital** is all the human-made resources used to produce goods and services. A **capitalist** is a person who owns capital and puts it to productive use. An **entrepreneur** combines land, labor, and capital resources to produce goods or offer services.

Capitalism is a **free enterprise system**—an economic system with private or corporate ownership of and investment in capital goods. Fundamental to it are private ownership, individual initiative, profit, and competition.

Under competitive conditions, the **laws of supply and demand** determine prices. These laws say that when supplies become more plentiful, prices tend to fall; when supplies become scarcer, prices tend to rise. Likewise, prices generally fall when demand drops; when demand increases, prices generally rise.

A company that is the only source of a product or service is a **monopoly.** A **trust** is a monopoly in which several corporations in the same industry combine to eliminate competition and regulate prices.

Laissez-faire theory holds that government should play a limited, hands-off role in society. The United States has a mixed economy—one in which private enterprise coexists with some governmental regulation of the economy.

THE BIG IDEA

In a capitalist economic system, private individuals or companies control the factors of production.

■ GRAPHIC SUMMARY: *Characteristics of Capitalism*

American capitalism is a mixed economy—private enterprise and governmental regulation coexist.

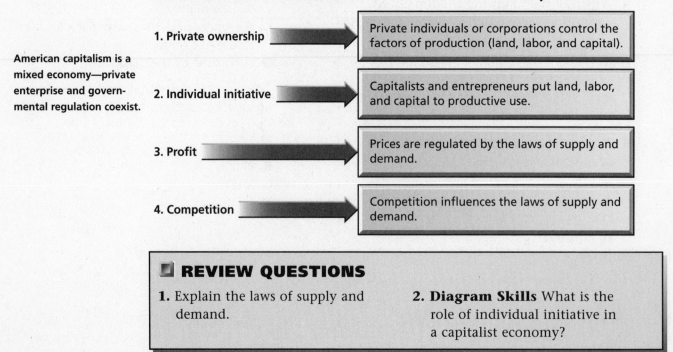

1. Private ownership → Private individuals or corporations control the factors of production (land, labor, and capital).

2. Individual initiative → Capitalists and entrepreneurs put land, labor, and capital to productive use.

3. Profit → Prices are regulated by the laws of supply and demand.

4. Competition → Competition influences the laws of supply and demand.

■ REVIEW QUESTIONS

1. Explain the laws of supply and demand.

2. **Diagram Skills** What is the role of individual initiative in a capitalist economy?

SOCIALISM

TEXT SUMMARY

Socialism is an economic and political philosophy that says the benefits of economic activity—wealth—should be fairly distributed throughout society. The theory began when, in 1848, Karl Marx and Friedrich Engels argued that the **proletariat**—the workers—were being so badly abused by the **bourgeoisie**—the capitalists—that the workers would surely overthrow the existing capitalistic system.

Socialist governments often favor nationalization—governmental control of certain businesses—and support of public welfare. Countries that provide extensive social services at little or no cost to the users are often called **welfare states.** These countries typically have high taxation because they need funds to pay for services.

A capitalist economy is a **market economy** because private individuals and companies make key economic decisions in the marketplace. A socialist economy is a **centrally planned economy** because government bureaucrats plan how the economy will develop.

Socialism's critics argue that it hinders individual initiative and makes the economy slow to utilize new technologies. Many critics believe that planning an economy is less efficient than letting the market control itself. They also claim that socialism gives workers no incentive to work hard because the government provides for their needs. Socialists respond that it is fairer and more moral to supply everyone with basic needs. They argue that socialism supplements political democracy with economic democracy. They also argue that socialism gives ordinary citizens more control over their daily lives.

THE BIG IDEA

In socialist countries, government plays a strong role in managing the economy and protecting workers' rights.

GRAPHIC SUMMARY: *The Development of Socialism*

The Problem
Marx and Engels viewed the proletariat—the workers—as being so badly abused by the bourgeoisie—the capitalists—that they were certain to overthrow the capitalistic system.

The Goal
The benefits of economic activity—wealth—should be fairly distributed throughout society.

The Result
Socialist governments typically favor governmental control of enterprises, support of public welfare, taxation, and a centrally planned economy.

Unlike capitalism, socialism seeks to distribute wealth more evenly throughout society.

REVIEW QUESTIONS

1. How does a centrally planned economy differ from a market economy?

2. Chart Skills What did Marx and Engels argue would happen to the capitalistic system?

 **SECTION 3** COMMUNISM

▣ TEXT SUMMARY

In the mid-1800s, Karl Marx developed the political, social, and economic theory of **communism,** which calls for the collective, or state, ownership of productive property. In any communist-run nation, the Communist Party holds all decision-making power in government and in the economy. Central planning results in bureaucrats planning the economy, usually with **five-year plans** that show how leaders want the economy to develop over that time. Also essential to communism are **collectivization**—the process of merging small, private farms into large, government-owned agricultural enter-prises—and state ownership of parts of the economy.

The Soviet Union became communist when Vladimir Lenin took control in 1917. Lenin's successor, Josef Stalin, intro-duced centralized planning run by a large agency called the **Gosplan.** Soviet communism lasted until 1991, when the Soviet Union fell apart. At that point Boris Yeltsin made radical changes in Russia, including the privatization of farms and factories. **Privatization** is the return of nationalized enterprises to private ownership.

In 1949 Mao Zedong founded the People's Republic of China as a communist nation. Mao's 1958 five-year plan was called the **Great Leap Forward.** It eliminated all elements of free enterprise and brought collective farms together into a larger unit called the **commune.** In 1978 Deng Xiaoping steered the country toward a market economy while maintaining a communist government.

In addition to China, communist governments continue to exist in Cuba, Vietnam, Laos, and North Korea.

 **THE BIG IDEA**

Communism is a political, social, and economic theory that calls for the collective, or state, ownership of productive property.

▣ GRAPHIC SUMMARY: *Characteristics of Communism*

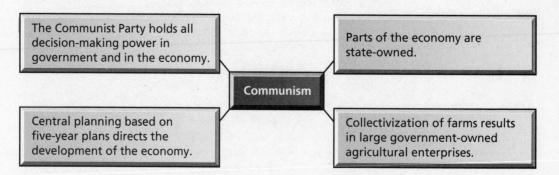

The Communist Party holds all decision-making power in government and in the economy.		Parts of the economy are state-owned.
	Communism	
Central planning based on five-year plans directs the development of the economy.		Collectivization of farms results in large government-owned agricultural enterprises.

Communism is a political, social, and economic theory that exists today in countries such as China.

▣ REVIEW QUESTIONS

1. In what ways do collectivization and privatization differ?

2. **Diagram Skills** What is the basis of central planning in communist economies?

Name _____ Class _____ Date _____

CHAPTER 23 *Test*

IDENTIFYING MAIN IDEAS

Write the letter of the correct answer in the blank provided. (10 points each)

_____ 1. Which is a factor of production?

    A. labor
    B. land
    C. capital
    D. all of the above

_____ 2. In a capitalist economy, the laws of supply and demand determine

    A. taxes.
    B. social services.
    C. prices.
    D. government involvement.

_____ 3. Capitalism is also called a

    A. command economy.
    B. welfare state.
    C. free social system.
    D. free enterprise system.

_____ 4. Karl Marx believed that the proletariat would overthrow

    A. the welfare state.
    B. the bourgeoisie.
    C. the lower class.
    D. industrialized countries.

_____ 5. Which economic system aims for equality of wealth?

    A. democracy
    B. capitalism
    C. socialism
    D. none of the above

_____ 6. Placing businesses under governmental control is called

    A. taxation.
    B. central planning.
    C. nationalization.
    D. privatization.

_____ 7. What kind of tax rates do socialist economies generally have?

    A. high
    B. low
    C. moderate
    D. nonexistent

_____ 8. Communism currently exists in all of the following countries except

    A. North Korea.
    B. Cuba.
    C. Russia.
    D. China.

_____ 9. The merging of small private farms into large government-owned enterprises is called

    A. collectivization.
    B. privatization.
    C. industrialization.
    D. nationalization.

_____ 10. Communism is

    A. a political theory.
    B. an economic theory.
    C. a social theory.
    D. all of the above

Governing the State of California

SECTION 1 THE CALIFORNIA STATE CONSTITUTION

■ TEXT SUMMARY

Each state has a written constitution, which is that state's supreme law. Each state constitution enshrines two principles: **popular sovereignty**, which means that the government's authority comes from the people, and **limited government**, which means that government only has specific powers.

California has had two constitutions—one passed in 1849, and the second passed in 1879. Since then, the California constitution has been amended more than 500 times. California's constitution sets forth a basic bill of rights, a structure for California government, some other basic details of government, and the procedures for amending the constitution.

An amendment to the California constitution will pass if it is ratified by two-thirds of both houses of the legislature, and is then approved by the voters. Voters may also propose amendments by means of the **initiative** process.

The California constitution is probably in need of reform, because it is lengthy and outdated. In addition, it does not maintain enough distinction between **fundamental law**—rules of basic and lasting importance—and **statutory law**.

> **THE BIG IDEA**
>
> The California constitution is the supreme law of the State; it sets out how California is governed.

■ GRAPHIC SUMMARY: California Constitution

State constitutions are much less flexible, and much more detailed, than the United States Constitution.

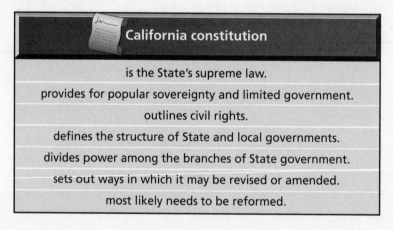

California constitution

is the State's supreme law.

provides for popular sovereignty and limited government.

outlines civil rights.

defines the structure of State and local governments.

divides power among the branches of State government.

sets out ways in which it may be revised or amended.

most likely needs to be reformed.

■ REVIEW QUESTIONS

1. Why is the California constitution in need of reform?

2. **Chart Skills** How can the California constitution be amended?

THE CALIFORNIA STATE LEGISLATURE

◼ TEXT SUMMARY

California has a bicameral legislature with two houses. The Senate, the upper house, has 40 members, while the lower Assembly has 80. In California, legislators must be 18, qualified to vote, have been a citizen of the United States and have lived in California for at least three years, and have been a resident of their district for at least one year. In practice, the requirements to win election are more extensive. Legislators are elected in November of even years. Both houses have term limits.

The California legislature can pass any law that does not conflict with Federal law or the state constitution. Among the most important of the California legislature's powers is the **police power**, which is the power to protect the health, safety, and welfare of the citizens.

The Assembly elects, from among its members, a Speaker to be its leader. The Senate elects a president pro tempore as its day-to-day leader. These leaders appoint the members of the legislative committees, who do most of the work on drafting, revising, and arguing over proposed laws. This process is similar to that used by the U.S. Congress.

California has two other methods for creating laws: the ballot initiative and the **referendum**. Under the initiative process, voters can propose legislation by signing a petition to have it placed on the ballot at the next election. Under a referendum, proposed laws are referred by the legislature to the voters for their ultimate approval.

> ### THE **BIG** IDEA
>
> The California legislature, the law-making body of California, is popularly elected and organized like Congress.

◼ GRAPHIC SUMMARY:
State Legislatures

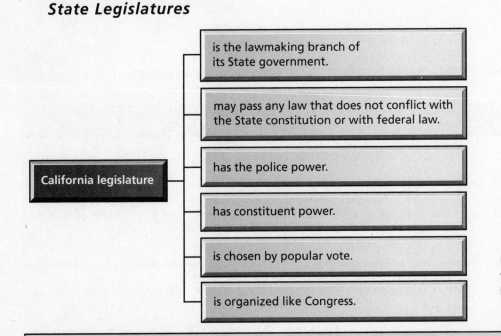

California legislature

- is the lawmaking branch of its State government.
- may pass any law that does not conflict with the State constitution or with federal law.
- has the police power.
- has constituent power.
- is chosen by popular vote.
- is organized like Congress.

Each State constitution defines the qualifications for its State legislature.

◼ REVIEW QUESTIONS

1. How are State legislators chosen?

2. Diagram Skills How are State legislatures limited in the kind of laws they can pass?

THE GOVERNOR AND STATE ADMINISTRATION

◪ TEXT SUMMARY

The chief executive officer in California is the governor. He or she is elected to a four-year term. The governor must be at least 18 years old, a qualified voter, and have been a citizen of the U.S. and resident of California for at least five years. As with the legislature, the informal requirements are more extensive, considering experience, qualifications, and the like.

If the governor resigns or dies in office, he or she is succeeded by the lieutenant governor. Governors may be removed from office by impeachment, in which the legislature charges and convicts the governor of a crime, or by **recall**. In a recall, voters attempt to remove the governor before the end of the term by signing a petition. If enough voters sign, a special election is held to vote the governor out of office.

The governor has many roles. The governor has the power to appoint and remove a number of officers of government, as well as to oversee their work. The governor also has the duty of preparing state's annual budget. The governor can veto laws and has the power to grant **clemency** to people convicted of crimes. The governor can also influence legislation, to make policy, and to promote California's interests in the outside world.

Many of California's other executives are also chosen by the voters. These include the Lieutenant Governor, the Secretary of State, the Controller, the Treasurer, the Attorney General, and the Board of Equalization.

> **THE BIG IDEA**
>
> The governor, the chief executive of California, is popularly elected, as are many other important State executive officers.

◪ GRAPHIC SUMMARY: *The Office of Governor*

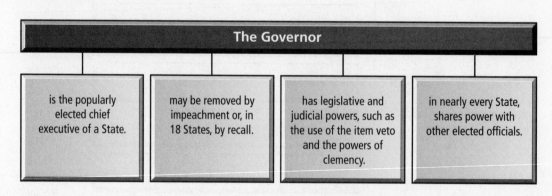

The Governor

| is the popularly elected chief executive of a State. | may be removed by impeachment or, in 18 States, by recall. | has legislative and judicial powers, such as the use of the item veto and the powers of clemency. | in nearly every State, shares power with other elected officials. |

California's governor has many powers, some of which he or she shares with other elected officials.

◪ REVIEW QUESTIONS

1. By what power may a governor reduce a person's sentence?

2. **Diagram Skills** What are two ways by which a governor may be removed from office?

IN THE COURTROOM

◼ TEXT SUMMARY

The law is the code of conduct governing society. It is made up of several forms. One of them, **common law,** is unwritten law that courts have developed over centuries from generally accepted ideas of right and wrong. Once a judge makes a decision in court, it becomes a **precedent,** or a guide to be used in similar cases.

The law can also be classified as criminal or civil. **Criminal law** involves cases brought against people accused of committing crimes, which are of two types. A **felony** is the greater crime, punishable by a heavy fine, imprisonment, or death. A **misdemeanor** is a lesser offense, punishable by a small fine or a short jail term. **Civil law** relates to disputes between private parties and between private parties

and government. It usually punishes people with fines.

A **jury** is a group of people selected to hear evidence and decide questions of fact in a court case. A grand jury is used only in criminal cases. It decides if the State has enough evidence to try someone. For minor cases, instead of a grand jury many States now use an **information,** which is a formal charge filed by the prosecutor. A petit, or trial, jury hears the evidence in a case and decides the disputed facts. In a **bench trial,** which is used in minor misdemeanor cases and civil proceedings, a judge decides the case without a jury.

> ### THE **BIG** IDEA
>
> State courts apply the forms of law that make up the code of conduct by which our society is governed.

◼ GRAPHIC SUMMARY: *The Role of State Courts*

State Courts
• govern based on the several forms of law, such as common law.
• set precedents with their rulings.
• divide court cases into two types: those of civil law and those of criminal law.
• use petit juries to hear evidence and decide questions of fact.
• may use grand juries in criminal cases or may, instead, use an information in minor criminal cases.
• may use bench trials to allow judges to hear minor misdemeanor and civil cases without a jury.

State courts decide disputes between private persons and between private persons and government.

◼ REVIEW QUESTIONS

1. What is the difference between a felony and a misdemeanor?

2. **Chart Skills** What kinds of cases may be heard in bench trials?

THE COURTS AND THEIR JUDGES

▣ TEXT SUMMARY

The California judicial system consists of three levels of courts: the superior courts, the courts of appeal, and the California Supreme Court. California's superior courts handle trials of all civil and criminal cases. There is one superior court in each of the 58 counties. Special departments of these courts are set up to handle family law, juvenile cases, traffic cases, and small claims.

When a party is not satisfied with the result of a Superior Court trial, he can take the case to the courts of appeal. There are six courts of appeal in California, one for each of six districts. These tribunals review cases that were tried in the superior courts to make sure that the law was correctly interpreted at the trial. Decisions of the courts of appeal can in turn be appealed to the California Supreme Court, the highest court in California. Their interpretation of California law is final.

Superior court judges in California are elected by voters to six-year terms. Appellate judges are appointed by the governor to a single twelve-year term; after that term, the judges face a retention election, in which the voters decide whether or not the judge should stay in office.

> ### THE **BIG** IDEA
>
> Judges for California courts, hear cases ranging from the minor to the most serious.

▣ GRAPHIC SUMMARY: *California State and Local Courts*

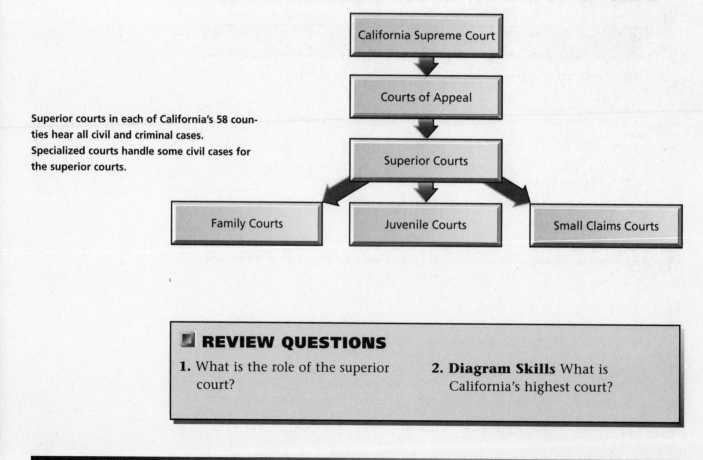

Superior courts in each of California's 58 counties hear all civil and criminal cases.
Specialized courts handle some civil cases for the superior courts.

California Supreme Court → Courts of Appeal → Superior Courts → Family Courts, Juvenile Courts, Small Claims Courts

▣ REVIEW QUESTIONS

1. What is the role of the superior court?

2. **Diagram Skills** What is California's highest court?

CHAPTER 24 *Test*

◼ IDENTIFYING MAIN IDEAS

Write the letter of the correct answer in the blank provided. (10 points each)

____ 1. The governor of California can be removed from office by a process called

    A. referendum

    B. initiative

    C. recall

    D. retention election

____ 2. The California state constitution can be amended if

    A. a majority of state senators passes the amendment.

    B. enough registered voters sign a petition.

    C. the California Supreme Court orders an amendment.

    D. two-thirds of both houses of the legislature approve the amendment, and a majority of California voters also approve.

____ 3. State legislatures are organized like

    A. the governor's office.

    B. Parliament.

    C. Congress.

    D. common law.

____ 4. In a criminal trial in California, the verdict is decided by

    A. the governor

    B. the board of supervisors

    C. a petit jury

    D. a three-judge panel

____ 5. The chief executive officer of every State is the

    A. manager.

    B. attorney general.

    C. governor.

    D. President.

____ 6. Supreme Court Justices in California are

    A. Elected in contested elections

    B. Appointed for life by the governor

    C. Appointed for only one term

    D. Appointed, then re-elected in uncontested elections

____ 7. Which type of law is unwritten?

    A. criminal law

    B. common law

    C. civil law

    D. precedent

____ 8. The governor of California has all of the following powers except

    A. the pocket veto

    B. the power to pardon convicted criminals

    C. the power to declare war

    D. the chief command of the California National Guard

____ 9. A California legislator must be

    A. at least 35 years old.

    B. a registered Republican or Democrat.

    C. a resident of the district the legislator represents.

    D. a native-born U.S. citizen.

____ 10. Which of these statements about the California lieutenant governor is FALSE?

    A. The lieutenant governor is the president of the Senate.

    B. If the governor resigns or dies in office, the lieutenant governor takes his place.

    C. The lieutenant governor is elected separately from the governor.

    D. The lieutenant governor has never been from a different party than the governor.

CHAPTER 25

Local Government and Finance

SECTION 1 CALIFORNIA COUNTIES, SPECIAL DISTRICTS, AND REGIONAL BODIES

■ TEXT SUMMARY

In most states, **counties** are the basic unit of local government. California has 58 counties. California has two types of counties: general law counties, and charter counties. General law counties follow state law in determining what structure their government has, whereas charter counties have opted to be governed according to another structure.

All California counties are governed by a Board of Supervisors that has the power to levy taxes and create local **ordinances**. In general law counties, there are five members of the Board of Supervisors; charter counties may use a different number. Each county also has a sheriff, a district attorney, and an assessor.

Special districts are local governmental bodies created to handle a specific task, such as managing water resources or operating an airport. Nationally, the most common special district is the school district. In California, school districts are managed by an elected school board with three to seven members. California also has a system of **regional bodies**, which are designed to handle problems that extend over a broader area than any county or city.

Native American tribal governments in California are recognized for 109 California tribes. These governments provide local services for Native American groups.

THE **BIG** IDEA

Forms of local government in California include counties and special districts.

■ GRAPHIC SUMMARY: *Forms of Local Government*

Form	Function	Governing Body
County	Administers State and county laws and maintains such things as jails, roads, schools, and tax collection.	Board of Supervisors
Special District	Performs governmental functions at the local level, such as administering schools and providing water, police protection, and bridge and park maintenance.	An elected board

In most places, local government is visible mainly in the day-to-day services that keep communities going.

■ REVIEW QUESTIONS

1. What role do a county's voters play in its management?

2. **Chart Skills** Name two functions of special districts.

CITIES AND METROPOLITAN AREAS IN CALIFORNIA AND THE NATION

◾ TEXT SUMMARY

In 1790 only 5% of Americans lived in urban areas. Today more than 80% of the U.S. population lives in cities or suburbs. In California, that figure is even higher, at 97%. Given this rural-urban shift, city government has become ever more important.

Each city in California has either a **mayor-council government** or a **council-manager government**. In a mayor-council government, the voters elect a mayor as the chief executive and a city council as the legislative body. In a council-manager government, the voters elect only a "weak" mayor and a city council, who then appoint a city manager to run the city. Three-fourths of California cities use a council-manager government.

Rapid growth of cities has emphasized the need for city planning. One common form of planning is **zoning**, in which a city is divided into zones in which the land can only be used for certain purposes. Zoning ordinances are an important function of city government. Other major functions of city government include providing police and fire protection, maintaining streets, collecting trash, managing sewer and water systems, and building parks and schools.

Urban growth has led to the rise of suburbs. Some government services are provided by both a city and its suburb, or by either and the county, at extra cost. California encourages local governments to cooperate by using councils of governments, which are regional districts set up to get other levels of government to work together.

THE **BIG** IDEA

Once primarily rural, the United States' population has become much more urban.

◾ GRAPHIC SUMMARY: *Aspects of City Government*

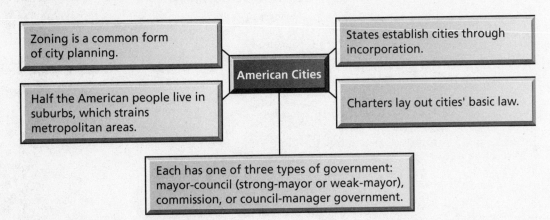

Zoning is a common form of city planning.

States establish cities through incorporation.

American Cities

Half the American people live in suburbs, which strains metropolitan areas.

Charters lay out cities' basic law.

Each has one of three types of government: mayor-council (strong-mayor or weak-mayor), commission, or council-manager government.

Cities, especially the larger ones, rely heavily on city government to provide extensive services.

◾ REVIEW QUESTIONS

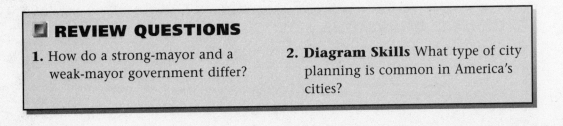

1. How do a strong-mayor and a weak-mayor government differ?

2. **Diagram Skills** What type of city planning is common in America's cities?

PROVIDING IMPORTANT SERVICES

■ TEXT SUMMARY

The state of California provides many services to citizens. It does so directly through State agencies and programs, and indirectly through local governments.

Education is one of the most important—and expensive—responsibilities of the State Local governments fund primary and secondary education, with some help from the State. The State also administers public university systems.

California works to promote citizens' welfare through many means. For example, the State funds public health programs such as **Medicaid,** which gives low-income families medical insurance. The State also contributes to **welfare**—cash assistance to the poor. This is an **entitlement** program—one in which anyone who meets the eligibility requirements is entitled to receive benefits. States promote public welfare in many other ways, including enforcing antipollution laws and protecting worker safety.

The State protects public safety by providing police units and correctional facilities for people convicted of State crimes. State corrections spending has greatly increased because of increased numbers of convicts and lengths of prison terms.

California also builds and maintains all highways and roads within its boundaries. California receives federal funds to assist with interstate highway maintenance.

State and local governments vary greatly in the services they offer. State budgets vary according to the degree of each State's **urbanization**—the percentage of State population living in cities of more than 250,000 people or in suburbs of more than 50,000 people.

> ### THE BIG IDEA
>
> State and local governments provide numerous expensive services for their citizens.

■ GRAPHIC SUMMARY: Services Provided by State and Local Government

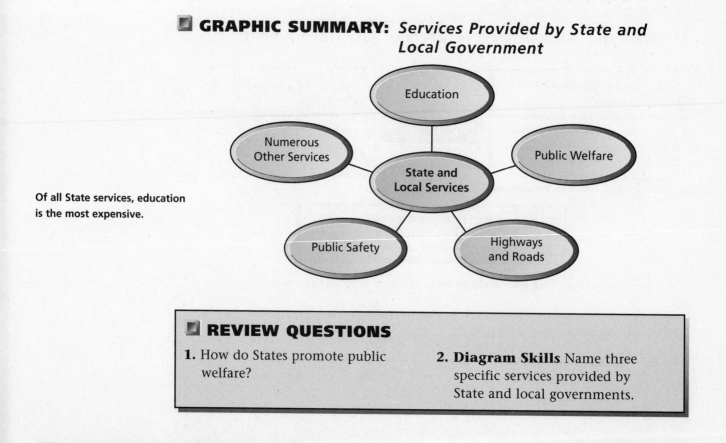

Education • Numerous Other Services • Public Welfare • State and Local Services • Public Safety • Highways and Roads

Of all State services, education is the most expensive.

■ REVIEW QUESTIONS

1. How do States promote public welfare?

2. **Diagram Skills** Name three specific services provided by State and local governments.

SECTION 4 FINANCING STATE AND LOCAL GOVERNMENT

◾ TEXT SUMMARY

State and local governments collect taxes to pay for the many services they provide. The Federal Constitution, the Fourteenth Amendment, and State constitutions limit taxing. State legislatures decide what taxes the State and localities will levy and at what rates.

A **sales tax** is a tax placed on the sale of various commodities; the purchaser pays it. Sales tax is a **regressive tax**—one that does not vary according to a person's ability to pay. Everyone in a State pays the same sales tax on any item.

An **income tax** is collected on the earnings of individuals and corporations. It provides about one third of State tax revenues. Individual income tax is usually a **progressive tax**—that is, the higher your income, the more tax you pay. Corporate income tax rates are usually a fixed percentage of income.

Local governments' largest source of income is the **property tax**—a levy on real property, such as land, or personal property, which includes bank accounts. The process of determining the value of the property to be taxed is called **assessment**. In California, property taxes raise much less money than income and sales taxes because Proposition 13 restricts property taxes. An **estate tax** is levied directly on the full value of an estate.

Other sources of State and local revenues include license taxes, document transfer taxes, and amusement taxes. State and local governments also receive nontax revenue through federal grants and publicly operated enterprises such as toll roads. A **budget** is a financial plan for the use of public money, personnel, and property.

THE BIG IDEA

States and local governments use taxes to collect the revenue that pays for services.

◾ GRAPHIC SUMMARY: *State and Local Taxes*

Type of Tax	What It Taxes
Sales tax	Various commodities
Income tax	Individual and corporate earnings
Property tax	Real or personal property
Estate tax	A full estate

The taxes levied by the State of California contributes substantially to State revenue.

◾ REVIEW QUESTIONS

1. What nontax sources provide State and local governments with revenue?

2. Chart Skills What type of tax is levied on corporate earnings?

CHAPTER 25 *Test*

◼ IDENTIFYING MAIN IDEAS

Write the letter of the correct answer in the blank provided. (10 points each)

____ 1. What is the largest unit of local government in most States?

    A. special district
    B. township
    C. county
    D. town

____ 2. A board of supervisors manages a

    A. special district.
    B. township.
    C. county.
    D. town.

____ 3. Which could a special district provide?

    A. school administration
    B. park maintenance
    C. police protection
    D. all of the above

____ 4. During its history, California's population has primarily

    A. shifted from rural to urban.
    B. remained rural.
    C. remained urban.
    D. shifted from urban to rural.

____ 5. The most widely used type of city government in California is

    A. commission government.
    B. council-manager government.
    C. mayor-council government.
    D. mayor-manager government.

____ 6. The practice of regulating the uses of property in a city's districts is called

    A. special districting.
    B. zoning.
    C. chartering.
    D. incorporation.

____ 7. One of California's most expensive responsibilities is

    A. highway construction and maintenance.
    B. public health.
    C. welfare.
    D. education.

____ 8. Cash assistance given to the poor is called

    A. childhood immunization.
    B. Medicaid.
    C. welfare.
    D. a federal grant.

____ 9. The Constitutional duty to prepare California's budget belongs to

    A. The state board of equalization
    B. The secretary of state
    C. The legislature
    D. The governor

____ 10. Which determines what taxes will be levied at the State and local level?

    A. State governments
    B. the Federal Government
    C. city governments
    D. county governments

GLOSSARY

A

absentee voting voting by people who are unable to get to their regular polling places on election day (p. 44)

acquit to find a person not guilty of an offense or crime (p. 64)

act of admission an act passed by Congress that approves the addition of a new State to the Union (p. 29)

adjourn to formally end a meeting or session (p. 55)

administration the government's many administrators and agencies (p. 82)

affirmative action the policy that requires organizations to take positive steps to overcome the effects of past discrimination (p. 114)

Albany Plan of Union Benjamin Franklin's 1754 plan for the 13 colonies to unite; the colonies did not accept it (p. 19)

alien a person who is not a citizen of the country in which he or she lives (pp. 102, 115)

ambassador a person appointed to represent the head of a nation in another country (p. 92)

amendment a change to a constitution or law (p. 25)

amnesty a general pardon for a group of lawbreakers (p. 80)

Anti–Federalist a person who opposed the ratification of the Constitution in 1787–1788 (p. 22)

appellate jurisdiction the power of a court to review decisions from lower courts (p. 97)

apportion to distribute, as with the seats in the House of Representatives (p. 56)

appropriate to assign money to a particular use (p. 63)

article one of the seven numbered sections into which the Constitution, after the Preamble, is divided (p. 24)

Articles of Confederation the document that set up the U.S. government that existed from 1781 to 1789 (p. 20)

assemble to gather with one another (p. 105)

assessment the process by which the value of property is determined for tax purposes (p. 136)

assimilation the process by which people of one culture merge into, and become part of, another culture (p. 112)

at-large a type of election in which all the voters in the State, rather than only part of them, vote for the candidate (p. 56)

attorney general the head of the Justice Department (p. 84)

autocracy a dictatorship in which one person holds unlimited political power (p. 15)

B

bail the money deposited with the court to assure that the accused person will appear at the time of trial (p. 110)

balance the ticket to choose a running mate who will strengthen a presidential candidate's chance of being elected by virtue of certain characteristics, such as ethnicity (p. 72)

ballot a device through which voters register their choices in an election (p. 44)

bankruptcy the legal action to release a person or a company from debt (p. 61)

bench trial a trial without a jury in which a judge makes the decisions (pp. 109, 130)

bicameral a legislature with two main parts, or houses (p. 18)

bill a proposed law (p. 68)

bill of attainder a law that inflicts punishment on a person or a group without benefit of a trial (p. 109)

Bill of Rights the Constitution's first ten amendments, which list rights the government must guarantee the people (pp. 25, 102)

bipartisan including members of both major political parties (pp. 33, 86)

blanket primary a primary in which every voter receives the same primary ballot—a long one containing the names of all contenders, regardless of party, for each nomination (p. 43)

block grant a federal grant used in a broadly defined area (p. 29)

bourgeoisie the Marxist name for capitalists (p. 123)

boycott the act of not buying someone's goods in order to force them to act a certain way (p. 19)

budget a spending plan with income and expenses (p. 136)

bureaucracy a structure or network of agencies, people, and rules through which the Federal Government operates (p. 82)

bureaucrat a person who works for a bureaucracy (p. 82)

C

Cabinet the key group of advisors to the President, made up of the heads of the executive departments (p. 26)

capital the human-made resources that people invest in producing goods and services (p. 122)

capital punishment the act of putting a convicted person to death for a crime (p. 110)

capitalist a person who owns capital and puts it to productive use (p. 122)

categorical grant a federal grant made for some specific, closely defined purpose and with conditions attached (p. 29)

caucus a group of people with similar political beliefs or membership in the same political party who select candidates to run for office (p. 43)

censure to formally condemn a civil officer's actions (p. 64)

centrally planned economy an economy whose development is planned by government bureaucrats (p. 123)

certificate the process used to send a case to the Supreme Court when a lower court is not clear about the procedure or the rule of law that should apply in the case (p. 99)

charter a document issued by a king granting colonists permission to set up a government (p. 18)

checks and balances a system that allows each branch of government to limit the other branches' power (p. 24)

chief administrator the President's role as director of government employees and manager of the budget (p. 71)

chief citizen the President's role as representative of all the people, working for the public interest (p. 71)

chief diplomat the President's role in setting policies and conducting relations with other countries (p. 71)

chief executive the President's role in carrying out the government's laws, policies, and programs (p. 71)

chief legislator the President's role in providing leadership to Congress (p. 71)

chief of party the President's role as the leader of his political party (p. 71)

chief of state the President's role as head of the government (p. 71)

citizen a person who owes allegiance to a state and is entitled to its protection (p. 115)

civil case a noncriminal case involving two or more people, businesses, and/or the government (p. 98)

civil law the part of the law not covered by criminal law that deals with disputes between private parties or between private parties and the government (p. 129)

civil liberties the protection of a person's safety, opinions, and property from government (p. 102)

civil rights the acts of the government that make constitutional guarantees work for people (p. 102)

civil service the people working for the Federal Government who are selected through competitive testing (p. 86)

civilian tribunal a court for the armed forces that is part of the judicial branch but entirely separate from the military (p. 100)

clemency powers of mercy that may be shown toward those convicted of a crime (pp. 80, 128)

closed primary a primary in which voting is open only to members of one political party (p. 43)

cloture a limit on debate (p. 69)

coattail effect the influence of a strong party candidate on other party candidates' success (p. 44)

cold war the period of more than 40 years during the latter half of the 20th century in which relations between the United States and the Soviet Union were tense and often hostile (p. 94)

colleague a coworker (p. 57)

collective security an arrangement in which nations form treaties for defense, promising that if one of them is attacked the others will come to its aid (p. 94)

collectivization the combining of small, private farms into giant, government-controlled farms (p. 124)

commander in chief the President's role as leader of the nation's armed forces (p. 71)

Commerce and Slave Trade Compromise an agreement at the Constitutional Convention forbidding Congress to tax the export of goods from any State or to act on the slave trade for a period of at least 20 years (p. 21)

commerce power the constitutional authority to regulate trade (p. 61)

committee chairman a member of Congress who heads one of the standing committees in each chamber (p. 66)

Committee of the Whole a committee consisting of all the members of a legislative body (p. 68)

common law the part of the law that is made up of judge-made decisions on right and wrong that over time became guides for later judicial decisions; it is nonstatutory law (p. 129)

commune the larger unit into which collective farms were brought together during China's Great Leap Forward (p. 124)

communism a type of government where one party has all the power to rule and controls the land and the economy (p. 124)

commutation the power to reduce a criminal sentence or fine (p. 80)

compromise the process of blending competing ideas to find a position acceptable to the most people (p. 16)

concurrent jurisdiction the sharing by federal and State courts of the power to hear certain cases (p. 97)

concurrent power a power shared between the National Government and the States (p. 28)

concurrent resolution a congressional measure that has the approval of both the House and the Senate but does not have the force of law (p. 68)

concurring opinion a statement written by one or more justices who agree with a Supreme Court decision to emphasize an idea or add a point to the majority opinion (p. 99)

confederation an alliance of states that creates a central government of very limited power; a joining of several groups for a common purpose (pp. 15, 19)

conference committee a temporary joint committee of Congress formed to develop a compromise bill when both houses have passed different versions of the same bill (p. 67)

Connecticut Compromise an agreement at the Constitutional Convention creating a two-house legislature; States received equal representation in one house, and representation based on population in the other house; also called the Great Compromise (p. 21)

consensus a general agreement among factions (pp. 33, 60)

constituency the people and interests the members of Congress represent (p. 57)

constitution a set of basic laws that both sets up a government and tells it what powers it has (p. 14)

constitutionalism the concept that government must be conducted according to constitutional principles (p. 24)

containment a basic principle of American foreign policy after World War II that called for preventing the spread of communism beyond where it already existed (p. 94)

content neutral the policy by which government may regulate assemblies on the basis of time, place, and manner but not on the basis of what might be said there (p. 105)

continuing resolution a measure passed by Congress that, if signed by the President, allows government agencies to continue spending based on last year's appropriations (p. 90)

continuous body a term applied to the Senate because all of its seats are never up for election at the same time (p. 57)

controllable spending the part of government spending about which Congress and the President can make choices (p. 90)

copyright the exclusive, legal right to reproduce, publish, and sell one's own creative work for a specific period of time (p. 62)

council-manager government the form of city government in which an elected council appoints a manager to serve as administrator (p. 133)

county a major unit of local government in most States (p. 132)

court-martial a court composed of military personnel for the trial of those accused of violating military law (p. 100)

criminal case a case in which a defendant is tried for committing an action declared by Congress to be a federal crime (p. 98)

criminal law the part of the law that identifies crimes or injuries against society and sets their punishments (p. 129)

Cultural Revolution the movement in China, led by Mao Zedong, in which the Red Guard attacked teachers, intellectuals, and anyone else who seemed to lack revolutionary fervor (p. 120)

custom duty a tax on imports or goods coming into the United States (p. 88)

D

de facto segregation segregation in fact, even if no law requires it (p. 113)

de jure segregation segregation with legal sanction (p. 113)

defendant in a court case, the person against whom the complaint is filed (p. 97)

deficit the amount of money government spends over its income (p. 89)

deficit financing spending more than is earned each year and borrowing the money to make up the difference (p. 61)

delegate a party representative to a meeting or convention (p. 19)

delegated power a power granted the National Government by the Constitution (p. 28)

democracy a form of government where supreme authority rests with the people (p. 14)

democratic consolidation building strong institutions to ensure a democracy survives (p. 119)

denaturalization the process by which naturalized citizens can involuntarily lose their citizenship (p. 115)

deportation a legal process in which aliens are legally required to leave the United States (p. 115)

détente a policy of purposefully attempting to improve relations that was used by the United States during the cold war (p. 94)

deterrence a U.S. policy of maintaining massive military strength to discourage attack on the United States or its allies (p. 94)

dictatorship a form of government where those who rule hold all political power and are not responsible to the people (p. 14)

diplomatic immunity a basic principle of international law—diplomats in a foreign country are not subject to its laws (p. 92)

direct popular election a plan that eliminates the electoral college and allows the people to vote directly for the President and Vice President (p. 75)

direct primary an election in which members of political parties choose their party's candidates for public office (p. 43)

direct tax a tax paid by the person it is imposed on (p. 61)

discharge petition a petition that enables members of Congress to force a bill that has remained in committee 30 days onto the floor for consideration (p. 68)

discrimination bias or unfairness (p. 108)

dissenting opinion a statement written by one or more justices who disagree with a Supreme Court majority opinion (p. 99)

district plan a plan for reform of the electoral college in which two of each State's electors would be chosen from the State at large and would cast their electoral votes in line with the result of the Statewide popular vote; the other electors would be elected, separately, in each of the State's congressional districts (p. 75)

divine right of kings the idea that God grants kings the right to rule (p. 118)

division of powers the sharing of power among branches or levels of government (pp. 15, 28)

docket a list of cases to be heard by a court (p. 98)

doctrine a principle or fundamental policy (p. 63)

domestic affairs the events happening in one's home country (p. 92)

double jeopardy a second trial for a crime for which the defendant has been found innocent; prohibited by the 5th Amendment (p. 109)

draft a government practice by which people are required to serve in the military (p. 93)

due process a constitutional guarantee that government will not deprive anyone of life, liberty, or property by unfair action (p. 107)

Due Process Clause the clause in the 5th and 14th Amendments of the U.S. Constitution that guarantees the government will treat people fairly (p. 102)

E

economic protest parties political parties working toward better economic times (p. 35)

electoral college the group of persons chosen from each State and the District of Columbia every four years to formally elect the President and Vice President (pp. 26, 73)

electoral votes the votes cast for vice-presidential and presidential candidates by the electoral college (p. 73)

electorate all of the people entitled to vote in an election (pp. 34, 38, 75)

eminent domain the constitutional authority the government can exercise to claim private land for public use (p. 62)

enabling act a law passed by Congress that gives approval to the people of a proposed State to write a constitution (p. 29)

encomienda feudal system in colonial Latin America (p. 118)

English Bill of Rights a document signed by the English king in 1689 that limited the king's power and guaranteed certain rights to the English people (p. 18)

engrossed printed in final form (a bill) (p. 68)

entitlement the benefits that federal law says people have a right to if they meet the eligibility requirements (pp. 90, 134)

entrepreneur an individual who combines the factors of production to produce goods or offer services (p. 122)

espionage the act of spying (p. 93)

Establishment Clause the 1st Amendment clause that says the government may not set up a religion or promote any one religion (p. 103)

estate tax a tax on the property and money of a person who has died (pp. 88, 135)

ex post facto law a law that makes an act illegal and punishes people who did that act before the law was passed (p. 109)

excise tax a tax on the manufacture, sale, or use of goods or services (p. 88)

exclusionary rule the rule that evidence gained illegally cannot be used against the person from whom it was seized (p. 108)

exclusive jurisdiction the power of the federal courts to be the only courts to hear certain cases (p. 97)

exclusive power a power exercised by only the National Government (p. 28)

executive agreement a pact made between the U.S. President and the head of another nation that does not require Senate approval (pp. 26, 79)

Executive Article Article II of the Constitution, which vests the executive power of the United States in the President (p. 77)

executive department one of the 14 traditional units of federal administration—also called Cabinet departments—by which much of the Federal Government's work is done (p. 84)

Executive Office of the President an umbrella agency under the President that is a complex organization of several separate agencies staffed by most of the President's closest advisors (p. 83)

executive order a rule the President makes for carrying out laws that itself has the force of law (p. 78)

executive power the power of a government to execute, enforce, and administer law (p. 14)

expatriation a legal act by which one gives up citizenship (p. 115)

expressed power a power listed in the Constitution (pp. 28, 60)

extradition a legal process by which police in one State return someone accused of a crime to the State filing charges (p. 30)

F

faction a dissenting group (p. 34)

factors of production the basic resources—land, labor, and capital—that are used to make all goods and services (p. 122)

failed state country without a working government (p. 119)

fascism a form of government with a strong, centralized dictatorship that puts the interest of the state over the individual (p. 118)

federal budget an estimate of the Federal Government's income and expenses over the coming year (p. 83)

federal government a government whose power is divided between a central government and local governments (p. 15)

federalism a system that divides governmental power between a central government and several regional governments (pp. 24, 28)

Federalist a person who favored the ratification of the Constitution in 1787–1788 (p. 22)

felony a serious crime with a heavy sentence or fine (p. 129)

feudalism a system of rule in which powerful lords divided up land among other, lesser lords (p. 117)

filibuster a tactic in which a senator uses the right to unlimited debate to talk continually against a bill (p. 69)

fiscal year a twelve-month period for a budget (p. 83)

five-year plan in a centrally planned economy, the plan by which leaders show how they want the economy to develop over a period of five years (p. 124)

floor leader the chief spokesperson for a party, who manages the business of the house and is responsible for ensuring the passage of legislation that the party seeks (p. 66)

foreign affairs the events that happen as part of a nation's relationship with other countries (p. 92)

foreign aid the economic and military aid that one nation provides to others as part of a plan to fulfill the provider nation's foreign policy goals (p. 95)

foreign policy the actions, positions, and statements of a government in its relations with other countries (p. 92)

formal amendment a change to the Constitution that alters the document's wording (p. 25)

Framers those colonial representatives who wrote the Constitution in 1787 (p. 21)

franchise the right to vote (p. 38)

franking privilege a benefit of members of Congress that allows them to mail letters and other materials postage-free (p. 58)

free enterprise system an economic system in which business is free to compete for profit without much government interference; another name for capitalism (pp. 16, 122)

Free Exercise Clause the 1st Amendment clause that says the government may not interfere in people's religious beliefs (p. 103)

Full Faith and Credit Clause the Article IV, Section 1 clause of the Constitution that states that all documentation and legal decisions made in one State are valid in all 50 States (p. 30)

fundamental law law of basic and lasting importance which may not easily be changed (p. 126)

G–H–I

gender gap the measurable differences between the partisan choices of men and women (p. 41)

general election the election in which candidates are chosen for office (p. 43)

gerrymandering the drawing of new boundaries for a district so a political party can gain more power (pp. 40, 56)

gift tax a tax on gifts of more than $10,000 (p. 88)

Gosplan the agency introduced to the Soviet Union by Stalin to institute centralized planning of the economy (p. 124)

government the institution through which a society makes and enforces public policies (p. 14)

government corporation an independent agency that is within the executive branch, subject to the President's direction and control, and was established by Congress to carry out certain business-like activities (p. 85)

grand jury a group of people called by a court to determine if there is enough evidence to accuse a person of a crime (p. 109)

grants-in-aid program the funds provided by the Federal Government to the States for a specific purpose (p. 29)

grass roots the "common" person; the "average" voter (p. 53)

Great Leap Forward China's five-year plan for 1958, which was a drastic attempt to modernize the country quickly by eliminating all elements of free enterprise (p. 124)

guarantee of association the right to associate with others to promote political, economic, and other social causes (p. 105)

hacienda large landholding in Latin America (p. 118)

hardliner People in power who oppose reforming repressive governments (p. 119)

hard money campaign money that is subject to regulation by the Federal Election Commission (p. 45)

heterogeneous composed of a mix of race, family, or kind (p. 112)

ideological party a political party based on a set of social, economic, and political beliefs (p. 35)

immigrant a person legally admitted as a permanent resident to a country (p. 112)

impeach to bring formal charges against a public official to remove the official from office (p. 64)

imperial presidency the concept that the President behaves like an emperor, taking strong actions without consulting Congress or seeking its approval—sometimes even acting in secrecy to evade or deceive Congress (p. 77)

implied power a power suggested by another power specifically listed in the Constitution (pp. 28, 60)

income tax a tax on personal or corporate income (p. 135)

incumbent the current officeholder (p. 34)

independent a voter not aligned with a political party (p. 41)

independent agency a government organization, formed outside existing departments, that conducts part of the government's business (p. 85)

independent executive agency an independent agency that does not have Cabinet status but that has thousands of employees, a substantial budget, and important public tasks to perform (p. 85)

independent regulatory commission an independent agency that is largely outside of presidential control and that regulates important aspects of the nation's economy (p. 85)

indictment a formal accusation by a grand jury (p. 109)

indirect tax a tax levied on one person, who passes the amount on to another (p. 61)

inferior court a court lower than the Supreme Court (p. 97)

informal amendment a change to the Constitution that does not alter the document's wording (p. 26)

information a formal charge filed by the prosecutor, without the action of a grand jury; used for most minor offenses (p. 129)

inherent power a power held simply because something is what it is; a National Government has certain powers because it rules a nation (pp. 28, 60)

initiative a petition process by which a certain percentage of voters can propose a statute, law, or amendment (p. 126)

injunction a court order to do or stop doing something (p. 40)

integration the process of bringing a group into equal membership in society (p. 113)

interest an additional amount of money charged by the person who loans money to another person (p. 89)

interest group a private organization whose members share certain views and work to shape public policy (pp. 48, 51)

interstate compact a formal agreement between or among the States (p. 30)

involuntary servitude forced labor (p. 108)

isolationism a policy of refusing to get involved in world affairs; the United States' basic foreign policy until World War II (p. 92)

J–K

Jim Crow law one of a body of laws that separate one group of people from another on the basis of race, aimed at African Americans (p. 113)

joint committee a committee made up of members of both the House and the Senate (p. 67)

joint resolution a measure agreed to by both the House and the Senate that has the force of law (p. 68)

judicial power the power of a government to interpret laws and to settle disputes within society (p. 14)

judicial review the power to decide whether a government action is in accord with the Constitution (p. 24)

jurisdiction a court's authority to judge a case (p. 97)

jury a body of persons selected according to law to hear evidence and decide questions of fact in a court case; in the American judicial system, there are grand juries and petit juries (p. 129)

jus sanguinis "the law of the blood"; the law that says anyone born to one U.S. citizen also is a U.S. citizen (p. 115)

jus soli "the law of the soil"; the law that says people born in the United States are automatically U.S. citizens (p. 115)

keynote address the opening address of a political party's national convention that sets the tone for the convention and for the presidential campaign (p. 74)

L

labor union an interest group in which members have the same kind of job or work in the same kind of business (p. 52)

laissez-faire theory the theory that government should play a very limited, hands-off role in society (p. 122)

laws of supply and demand an economic principle that states that price is determined by an item's availability and by the demand for the item (pp. 16, 122)

legal tender any kind of money that a creditor must accept in payment of a debt (p. 61)

legislative power the power of a government to make law and frame public policies (p. 14)

libel an untrue written statement that can damage a person's reputation (p. 104)

liberal constructionist a person who favors broad interpretation of the Constitution (p. 60)

limited government the belief that governments have only the powers given them by the people (pp. 18, 126)

line agency an agency of the administration that performs the tasks for which the organization exists (p. 82)

line-item veto the executive power to delete any part of a bill rather than disapprove of the entire bill (p. 80)

literacy the ability to read or write (p. 39)

lobbying the act of trying to persuade government officials to support certain causes or beliefs (p. 53)

M–N–O

Magna Carta an English document from 1215 in which the English king first agreed to the idea of limited government (p. 18)

major party a dominant political party with significant support; Republicans and Democrats in American politics (p. 32)

majority opinion a written statement explaining a court's official decision (p. 99)

mandate a claim by an elected official that voters are giving permission by their support to act on campaign promises (p. 48)

market economy an economy based on capitalism (p. 123)

mass media those means of communication that reach large, widely dispersed audiences simultaneously (pp. 47, 77)

mayor-council government a form of city government in which a mayor (some with many powers and some with few) and a city council form the executive and legislative branches (p. 133)

Medicaid a program jointly administered by the States and the Federal Government that provides medical insurance to low-income families (p. 134)

medium a way of communicating (p. 49)

mercantilism economic policy that controlled trade to bring more gold and silver into a country (p. 117)

minister a British cabinet member (p. 120)

minor party one of the less widely supported political parties in a governmental system (p. 33)

Miranda Rule the list of rights which a suspect must be read before police questioning (p. 109)

misdemeanor a minor crime (p. 129)

mixed economy an economy in which private enterprise exists in combination with a considerable amount of government regulation and promotion (p. 16)

monopoly a firm that is the only source of a product or service (p. 122)

multiparty a political system in which three or more major parties compete (p. 33)

national bonus plan a plan for reform of the electoral college in which it is kept mostly intact and the winner-take-all feature weights in favor of the popular vote (p. 75)

national convention the meeting at which a party's delegates vote for their presidential and vice-presidential candidates (p. 74)

naturalization a legal process by which a citizen of one country becomes a citizen of another country (pp. 62, 115)

Necessary and Proper Clause Article I, Section 8, Clause 18 of the Constitution; it gives Congress the power to make all laws "necessary and proper" for the execution of its duties (p. 63)

New Jersey Plan a blueprint for government backed by the small States at the Constitutional Convention (p. 21)

nomination the proposing of candidates for office (p. 43)

nonpartisan election an election in which candidates are not identified by party labels (p. 43)

oath of office the oath sworn by the President on the day he takes office, which gives him the power to execute the law (p. 78)

off-year election a congressional election held in the even-numbered years between presidential elections (pp. 41, 56)

oligarchy a dictatorship in which a small, usually self-appointed elite holds the power to rule (p. 15)

one-party system a political system in which only one party can win an election (p. 33)

open primary a primary in which any registered voter may cast a vote (p. 43)

opinion leader a person who has a big influence on what other people think (p. 47)

ordinance power the President's power to issue executive orders, given by the Constitution and acts of Congress (p. 78)

original jurisdiction the authority to be the first court to hear and judge a case (p. 97)

oversight function the process by which Congress, through its committees, checks to see if various agencies in the executive branch are working effectively and acting in line with the policies that Congress has set by law (p. 58)

P–Q

pardon the release from the punishment or legal consequences of a crime (p. 80)

parliamentary government a government whose executive branch is chosen and controlled by its legislative branch (p. 15)

parochial church related (p. 103)

partisan a role a legislator demonstrates when he or she votes on issues based on political party loyalty (p. 58)

partisanship a firm allegiance to a political party that is the basis for government action (p. 32)

party caucus a closed meeting of the members of each party in each house (p. 66)

party identification a loyalty to a political party (p. 41)

party in power the party that controls the executive branch—the presidency at the national level or the governorship at the State level (p. 32)

patent a license granting an inventor the right to manufacture and sell his or her invention for a specific period of time (p. 62)

patronage the giving of jobs to supporters and friends (p. 86)

payroll tax a tax that is withheld from a worker's pay by his or her employer and sent to the government (p. 88)

peer group the group of people with whom a person regularly associates, including friends, classmates, and coworkers (p. 47)

perjury lying under oath (p. 64)

persona non grata the title given to officials when the President recalls them from a foreign country because he is displeased with that country's conduct (p. 79)

Petition of Right a document signed by the English king in 1628 restating the basic ideas of limited government and the king's obedience to the law (p. 18)

picketing the patrolling of a business site by workers on strike to persuade others not to deal with that employer (p. 104)

plaintiff in a court case, the person who files suit (p. 97)

platform the stated basic principles of a political party (p. 74)

pluralistic society a culture made up of many distinct groups (p. 33)

plurality the largest number of votes cast for an office in an election (p. 33)

pocket veto an informal veto that occurs when Congress adjourns before the ten-day period in which the President must act; without a presidential signature, the bill in a sense dies while "waiting in a pocket" (p. 69)

police power the power of States to act to protect and promote the public health, safety, morals, and welfare (pp. 107, 127)

political action committee (PAC) the political arm of a special interest group that has a major stake in public policy (p. 45)

political asylum the right to a safe haven for those persecuted in their home countries (p. 93)

political efficacy a person's sense of his or her own influence or effectiveness in politics (p. 41)

political party a group of people who try to control government by winning election and holding public office (p. 32)

political socialization a process by which a person develops attitudes and opinions about politics (p. 41)

politico a role a legislator shows when he or she votes on issues based on a blend of conscience, political party influence, and constituent opinions (p. 58)

poll books lists of all registered voters in each precinct (p. 39)

poll tax a tax one must pay to qualify for voting (p. 39)

polling place the actual location or building at which voters cast ballots (p. 44)

popular sovereignty the belief that all government power comes from the people and that government acts only with the consent of the people (pp. 19, 126)

Preamble the introduction to the Constitution (p. 24)

precedent the earlier judicial decisions that become guides in making later judicial decisions (pp. 99, 129)

precinct a local voting district (pp. 36, 44)

preclearance the first approval of a change to an existing election law by the Department of Justice (p. 40)

president of the Senate the officer who oversees the Senate; the Vice President of the United States holds this position (p. 66)

president *pro tempore* the senator who oversees the Senate's sessions when the Vice President is not there (p. 66)

presidential electors the persons elected by the voters of each State to represent that State in the formal process of choosing the President and Vice President (p. 73)

presidential government a government whose legislative and executive branches are separate (p. 15)

presidential primary the election in which voters of a State indicate which of a political party's presidential candidates they prefer to be its nominee (p. 74)

presidential succession the manner in which a vacancy in the office of President is filled (p. 72)

Presidential Succession Act of 1947 an act that puts the Speaker of the House and then the president *pro tempore* of the Senate next in the line of succession after the Vice President (p. 72)

presiding officer a member of a body, such as the House or Senate, who acts as the body's chairperson (p. 20)

preventive detention the law under which federal judges can order that accused felons be held without bail when there is good reason to believe that they will commit another serious crime before trial (p. 110)

prior restraint the limitation of spoken or written words and ideas before they are expressed (p. 104)

privatization the returning of nationalized enterprises to private ownership (p. 124)

Privileges and Immunities Clause the Article IV, Section 2 clause of the Constitution that states that no State can draw unreasonable distinctions between its own residents and those persons who happen to live in other States (p. 30)

probable cause the reasonable grounds to believe a crime has been committed (p. 108)

procedural due process that part of due process of law that requires that government procedures be fair (p. 107)

process of incorporation the process by which the Supreme Court has incorporated most of the guarantees in the Bill of Rights into the 14th Amendment's Due Process Clause (p. 102)

progressive tax a tax whose rates are based on the ability of the person to pay; in other words, the higher one's income, the greater one's tax rate (pp. 88, 135)

project grant a federal grant made to a State, locality, or private agency that applies for it (p. 29)

proletariat the Marxist name for workers in a capitalist economy (p. 123)

propaganda the ideas spread by one group to influence the ideas of others (p. 53)

property tax a tax on real property—land and buildings—and/or personal property (p. 136)

proportional plan a plan for reform of the electoral college in which each presidential candidate would receive the same share of the State's electoral vote as he or she received in the State's popular vote (p. 75)

proportional representation a Democratic Party rule that any candidate who wins at least 15 percent of the votes cast in a primary gets the number of State Democratic convention delegates that corresponds to his or her share of that primary vote (p. 74)

proprietary a colony in North America organized by a proprietor—a person with a grant of land from England's king (p. 18)

prorogue the presidential power to adjourn a congressional session when the houses cannot agree on a date for adjournment (p. 55)

public affairs the events and issues that concern the people at large (pp. 47, 51)

public agenda the societal problems that political leaders and citizens agree need government attention (p. 49)

public debt the total amount of money borrowed but not paid back by the Federal Government, plus the interest on this borrowed money (pp. 61, 89)

public opinion the opinion held by most people about a certain issue (p. 47)

public opinion poll a survey to collect opinions about government and politics (p. 48)

public policy a plan of action to support or reach a government goal (pp. 14, 51)

public-interest group an interest group that supports general causes that affect all Americans (p. 52)

purge the removal from the poll books of names of voters who are no longer eligible (p. 39)

quasi-judicial having certain judicial-like powers (p. 85)

quasi-legislative having certain legislative-like powers (p. 85)

quorum the minimum number of members in attendance to conduct official business; generally, a majority of total membership (pp. 22, 68)

quota a rule requiring that a certain number of jobs be set aside for a certain group of people (p. 114)

quota sample a sample deliberately constructed to reflect several of the major characteristics of a given "universe" (p. 48)

R

random sample a group of people to be surveyed, who were selected by chance from the survey's "universe" (p. 48)

ratify to give final approval to a constitution (p. 20)

reapportion to divide up the total number of seats in the House of Representatives based on the population in each State and district (p. 56)

recall a petition procedure by which voters may remove an elected official from office before the completion of his or her regular term (p. 128)

recognition the diplomatic practice by which one nation's government acknowledges the legal existence of another nation's government (p. 79)

redress a repayment to satisfy a claim (p. 100)

referendum the process by which a proposed law is referred to the voters for final approval or rejection (p. 127)

refugee a person who leaves his or her home to seek refuge from war, persecution, or other danger (p. 112)

regional security alliance an alliance between the United States and another country that is based on a mutual defense treaty that agrees to the two countries taking collective action to meet aggression in a particular part of the world (p. 95)

register a list of those applicants qualified for employment by having passed the Office of Personnel Management's tests (p. 86)

registration the process of identifying oneself to election officials so one can vote (p. 39)

regressive tax a tax whose rate is the same for everyone; it does not take into account the taxpayer's ability to pay (pp. 88, 135)

repeal to recall a regulation, such as a trade regulation (p. 19)

representative government the type of government in which the work of government is done by elected officials (p. 18)

reservation land reserved for a Native American group (p. 112)

reserved power a power set aside for the 50 States (p. 28)

resolution a congressional measure passed by one of the houses of Congress that does not have the force of law (p. 68)

revenue sharing from 1972 to 1987, a federal monetary aid program in which Congress gave an annual share of the federal tax revenue to the States and their cities, counties, and townships (p. 29)

reverse discrimination the concern of critics of affirmative action that preference to a minority group leads to discrimination against the majority group (p. 114)

rider a proposed law, with little chance of enactment on its own, that is added to a bill likely to be approved (p. 68)

right of legation the right of every nation, by international law, to send and receive diplomatic representatives (p. 92)

rule of law the concept that government and its officers are always subject to—never above—the law (p. 24)

runoff primary a primary in which the top two vote-getters in the first primary face one another (p. 43)

S

sales tax a tax paid by the purchaser on the sale of certain goods (p. 135)

sample a part of a scientific polling in which a small group of people represent the total group (p. 48)

search warrant a court order authorizing the search of a suspect's person or property (p. 107)

secretary the head of each of the Federal Government's executive departments (p. 84)

sectionalism a political devotion to the interests of a particular region (p. 34)

sedition the promotion of resistance to lawful authority (p. 104)

seditious speech the advocating, or urging, of conduct that attempts to overthrow the government by force or to disrupt its lawful activities by violent acts (p. 104)

segregation the separation or isolation of one group of people from the rest of the population in any area of life (p. 113)

select committee a temporary committee in the House or Senate, set up to perform a specific task in a specified time (p. 67)

senatorial courtesy the custom by which the Senate will not approve a presidential appointment opposed by a senator of the President's party from the State in which the appointee would serve (p. 26)

seniority rule the custom in Congress of making the "ranking member" (the member who has been there the longest) of the majority party on a standing committee its chairman (p. 66)

separate-but-equal doctrine the doctrine once upheld by the Supreme Court that stated that if the separate facilities for African Americans were equal to those for whites, then segregation did not violate the Constitution's Equal Protection Clause (p. 113)

separation of powers a system that divides governmental power among three separate, independent branches—the executive, the legislative, and the judicial (p. 24)

serf worker tied to the land he or she farmed (p. 117)

session a meeting of a group to accomplish its goals (p. 55)

shadow cabinet in Britain, the team of potential cabinet members appointed by each opposition party to be ready to run the government if an opposition party gains a majority (p. 117)

shield law a law that gives reporters some protection against having to disclose their sources or reveal other confidential information in legal proceedings (p. 104)

single-interest group an interest group formed to focus on one issue (p. 53)

single-issue party a political party that promotes the adoption of one public policy issue (p. 35)

single-member district an electoral district for which voters elect one person for each office (pp. 33, 56)

slander an untrue spoken statement that can damage a person's reputation (p. 104)

socialism an economic and political philosophy that says the benefits of economic activity—wealth—should be equitably distributed throughout a society, which can be achieved through the collective ownership of the most important means of producing and distributing goods and services (p. 123)

softliner person in power who supports reform to protect the government (p. 119)

soft money money given to State and local party organizations for such "party-building activities" as voter registration, get-out-the-vote drives, party mailings and advertisements, and "voter education" (p. 45)

sound bite a short, attention-getting message from a candidate that is often used on TV news programs (p. 49)

sovereign having the supreme power to rule (p. 14)

Speaker of the House the officer who oversees the House of Representatives (p. 66)

special district an independent unit created to perform one or more related governmental functions at the local level (p. 132)

special session a session of Congress that meets under emergency circumstances (p. 55)

splinter party a political party that splits from one of the major parties, typically supporting a political leader who did not receive the major party's nomination (p. 35)

split-ticket voting the act of voting for candidates of more than one party in the same election (pp. 36, 41)

spoils system the practice of giving government offices and other favors to friends and political allies (p. 86)

staff agency an agency of the administration that serves in a support capacity (p. 82)

standing committee a permanent committee in one of the houses of Congress (p. 67)

state a group of people living in a defined area, with a system of government that answers to no higher authority (p. 14)

statutory law laws passed by a legislature (p. 126)

straight-ticket voting the act of voting for only the candidates of the political party with which one identifies (p. 41)

straw vote an unscientific poll in which any large group of people are asked the same question (p. 48)

strict constructionist a person who favors a narrow interpretation of the Constitution to safeguard States' rights (p. 60)

subcommittee a subdivision of a committee (p. 68)

subpoena a court order for a person to appear in court or to produce documents or other requested materials (p. 64)

subsidy a gift of money, usually from a government (p. 44)

substantive due process that part of due process of law that requires that government procedures be fair (p. 107)

successor the next person in line for an office (p. 64)

suffrage the right to vote (p. 38)

surplus the amount of money that the government earns over its expenses (p. 89)

symbolic speech the act of expressing ideas through conduct or appearance (p. 104)

T–U

tax a sum of money the government charges its people to pay for government expenses (p. 61)

tax return a document that states a taxpayer's income, deductions, exemptions, and tax due (p. 88)

term the length of time an official stays in office (p. 55)

Three-Fifths Compromise the agreement at the Constitutional Convention allowing slave States to include three-fifths of their slaves when counting their populations (p. 21)

trade association an interest group formed with people who work in the same kind of business (p. 52)

transient a person living in a State for only a short time (p. 39)

treason an act defined in the Constitution as levying war against the nation or supporting its enemies (p. 110)

treaty a formal agreement between nations (pp. 26, 79)

trust a monopoly in which several corporations in one industry combine to eliminate competition and regulate prices (p. 122)

trustee a role a legislator shows when he or she votes on issues based on good judgment, conscience, and the bill's merits (p. 58)

two-party system a political system in which only candidates of two political parties have a good chance of winning (p. 33)

UN Security Council the organization within the United Nations that bears the UN's major responsibility for maintaining international peace (p. 95)

unconstitutional not permitted by the Constitution (p. 24)

uncontrollable spending the part of government spending that Congress and the President have no power to change directly (p. 90)

unicameral a legislature with one major part, or house (p. 18)

unitary government a form of government with power located in a single central agency (p. 15)

urbanization the amount of a State population that lives in large cities or suburbs (p. 134)

V–Z

vassal a lord who was loyal to a more powerful lord (p. 117)

veto the power of the President to stop a bill from becoming law by not signing it and returning it to Congress (pp. 24, 69)

Virginia Plan a blueprint for government, presented at the Constitutional Convention, that was favored by the most populous States (p. 21)

ward a local unit of party organization, often used for city council elections (p. 36)

welfare cash assistance given to the poor by States (p. 134)

welfare state a country in which basic services are provided for everyone (p. 123)

whip an assistant floor leader in one house of Congress (p. 66)

winner-take-all a primary at which the candidate who wins the preference vote automatically wins the support of all the delegates chosen at the primary (p. 74)

writ of assistance a blanket search warrant used in colonial times by British customs officials to invade private homes to search for smuggled goods; the basis for the 4th Amendment (p. 108)

writ of certiorari an order by the Supreme Court directing a lower court to send a case's record for review (p. 99)

writ of habeas corpus a court order demanding that a prisoner be brought before the court so the detaining officer can show why the prisoner should not be released (p. 109)

zoning the practice of dividing an area into districts to regulate how the land is used (p. 133)

INDEX

A

accused persons, rights of, 109–110
act of admission, 29
Acting President, U.S., 72
Adams, John, 34, 73
administration, bureaucracy and, 82
affirmative action, 114
African Americans, 34; discrimination and, 112–113; voting rights and, 38, 40. *See also slavery.*
agency, bureaucracy and, 82; independent, 85; independent executive, 85
Agriculture, Department of, bureaucracy and, 84
Albany Plan of Union, 19
alien, 102, 115
alliances, defense, 95
ambassadors, 79, 92
Amendment, First, 103–105
Amendment, Second, 108
Amendment, Third, 108
Amendment, Fourth, 108
Amendment, Fifth, 107, 109
Amendment, Eighth, 110
Amendment, Twelfth, 73
Amendment, Thirteenth, 108
Amendment, Fourteenth, 102–105, 107, 108, 113
Amendment, Fifteenth, 38
Amendment, Nineteenth, 38
Amendment, Twenty-second, 71
Amendment, Twenty-fourth, 38
Amendment, Twenty-fifth, 72
Amendment, Twenty-sixth, 38
amendments, constitutional, 8, 25–26; formal, 25; informal, 26; power of Congress in, 26; process of, 25–26. *See also Bill of Rights, U.S.; specific amendments.*
amnesty, 80
Annapolis Convention, 20

B

bail, 110
ballots, types of, 44
bankruptcy, 61
bench trial, 109
bicameralism, 18; in Congress, 55
bill of attainder, 109
Bill of Rights, English, 18
Bill of Rights, U.S., 25, 102. *See also amendments, constitutional.*
bills, 68–69. *See also legislation, congressional.*
block grants, 29
borrowing powers, of Federal Government, 89; interest, 89
bourgeoisie, 123
boycott, 19
Britain. *See Great Britain.*
Brown v. Board of Education of Topeka, 113
budget, federal, 83; approval process of, 90; President and, 90
bureaucracy, federal, 82–86; definition of, 82; hierarchical structure of, 82; parts of, 82–86

C

Cabinet, U.S., 26; bureaucracy and, 84
calendars, of House of Representatives, 68

Anti-Federalists, 22, 34
appeal, 97–100
appellate jurisdiction, federal courts and, 97; State courts and, 131
appointing powers, of President, 78
appropriations, 63, 90
arms, right to keep and bear, 108
Articles of Confederation, 20, 22
Asian Americans, 112
at-large elections, 56
attorney general, State, 129
attorney general, U.S., 84
authorities, bureaucracy and, 82
autocracy, 15

California State government, 126–130, 134–135; budget, 135; constitutions of, 126; court systems of, 129–130; expenses of, 134–135; kinds of laws of, 129; legislatures of, 127; nontax revenues, 135; paying for, 135; revenues, 135; services provided by, 134; taxes, 135
campaigns, political. *See political campaigns.*
capitalism, 122; characteristics of, 122; factors of production, 122; free enterprise system and, 122
capital punishment, 110
categorical grants, 29
caucus, 43
caucus, party, choosing delegates to national convention, 74; nomination by, 66
census, in reapportionment, 56
Central Intelligence Agency (CIA), foreign affairs and, 93
centrally planned economy, 123
charter colonies, 18
checks and balances, 24
chief administrator, President as, 71
chief citizen, President as, 71
chief diplomat, President as, 71, 79
chief executive, President as, 71, 77–78
chief legislator, President as, 71, 80
chief of party, President as, 71
chief of state, President as, 71
China, relations with U.S., 94
citizenship, American, 115; by birth, 115; expatriation, 115; jus sanguinis, 115; jus soli, 115; naturalization, 115; as a voting qualification, 38–39
city government, 133; commission form of, 133; council-manager form of, 133; mayor-council form

of, 133; strong-mayor type, 133; weak-mayor type, 133; zoning powers of, 133
city manager, 133
civil law, 129
civil liberties, 102
civil rights, 113–114; freedoms of, 102; voting rights and, 38, 40. *See also minorities.*
Civil Rights Acts, of 1957, 40; of 1960, 40; of 1964, 40, 113–114; of 1965, 40; of 1968, 114
Civil Rights Commission, 40
Civil Service, 86
Civil Service Act of 1883, 86
clemency, powers of governor, 128; powers of President, 80
closed primary, 43
cloture rule, 69
coalition, 117
coattail effect, 44
cold war, 94
collective security, definition of, 94
collectivization, 124
commander in chief, President as, 71, 77, 79, 92
commerce, power of Congress, 61
Commerce, Department of, bureaucracy and, 84
Commerce and Slave Trade Compromise, 21
commission, bureaucracy and, 82; of city government, 133; independent regulatory, 85. *See also commission by name.*
committee, congressional, 66–69; bills in, 68–69; conference, 67; joint, 67; select, 67; standing, 67. *See also specific names of committees.*
Committee of the Whole, House, 68
common law, 129
communism, 124; China and, 124; containment of, 94; fall of, 124; Marx's theory of, 124; Soviet Union and, 119

labor union, 52
laissez-faire theory, 122
Latin America, 95, 118, 120
legal tender, 61
legislation, congressional, committee stage of, 67–69; conference committee stage, 67; in House of Representatives, 68; introduction in House, 68; placement on calendar, 68; President acting on, 69; President's choices and review of, 80; resolutions and, 68; riders added to, 68; Rules Committee stages of, 67; in Senate, 69; subcommittee stage of, 68
legislative branch, 15, 24; working with executive, 15
legislative courts. *See special courts.*
legislative powers, of governor, 128; of President, 80
legislatures, State, 127; bicameralism in, 127; organization of, 127; referendum in, 127; unicameralism in, 127
Lenin, Vladimir, 119
libel, 104
liberal constructionists, 60; versus strict, 60
lieutenant governor, 128
limited government, 18, 24
line-item veto, 80
literacy, and voting, 39
lobbying, 53
magazines, 49
Magna Carta, 18
major party, 32–33
majority opinion, 99
majority rule, 16
Management and Budget, Office of (OMB), 90
mandate, 48
Mao Zedong, 124
Marbury v. *Madison,* 99
market economy, 123
Marx, Karl, 123–124
Maryland, Annapolis Convention, 20
mass media, definition of, 47, 77; impact on politics, 77; measurement of public opinion through, 47. *See also specific media.*
McCulloch v. *Maryland,* 63
Medicare, 88

Merit Systems Protection Board, 86
Mexico, government of, 120
military powers, of President, 79
minimum wage, history of, 6
minor party, 33, 35
minorities, diversity and discrimination, 112; voting rights of, 38, 40. *See also civil rights.*
minority rights, 16
Miranda Rule, 109
misdemeanor, 129
monarchy, British, 120
Monroe Doctrine, 94
Mount Vernon Convention, 20
multi-party system, 33

N–O

National Aeronautics and Space Administration (NASA), defense policy and, 93
national chairperson, 36
national committee, 36
national convention, 36
national debt. *See public debt.*
National Drug Control Policy, Office of, 83
National Government. *See Federal Government.*
National Security Council (NSC), 83
Native Americans, 112; reservations of, 112
naturalization, American citizenship and, 115; definition of, 62, 115
Necessary and Proper Clause, 63
New England confederation, 19
New Jersey Plan, 21
New York (State), ratification of Constitution, 22
newspapers, 49
Nixon, Richard, 34
nomination, political, 43; in caucuses, 43; in conventions, 43; by direct primary, 43; by petition, 43; by self-announcement, 43
nonlegislative powers, congressional, 64
North Atlantic Treaty Organization (NATO), 95
North Dakota, lack of voter registration in, 39

obscenity, 104
Office of —. *See offices by name.*
office-group ballot, 44
off-year elections, 41
Old-Age, Survivors, and Disability Insurance (OASDI), 88, 90
oligarchy, 15
one-party system, 33
open primary, 43
opinion leader, 47
ordered government, 18
ordinance power, 78
original jurisdiction, federal courts and, 97–99

P–Q

pact. *See executive agreement.*
pardon, by President, 80
Parliament, British, 117
parliamentary government, 15
parole, by governor, 129
party identification, factors affecting, 41
party-column ballot, 44
patent, 62
payroll tax, 88
Pendleton Act, 86
Personnel Management, Office of, civil service and, 86
petition, nomination by, 43
Petition of Right, 18
Philadelphia Convention. *See Constitutional Convention.*
Philippines, the, foreign aid to, 95
picketing, 104
plaintiff, 97
platform, political party, 74
Plessy v. *Ferguson,* 113
pluralistic society, 33
pocket veto, 69, 80
police powers, 107, 127; due process and, 107
political action committees (PACs), 45; contributors to candidates, 53
political campaigns, disclosure of financial information, 45; funding of, 45; limits on contributions to, 45; spending for, 45
political parties, 32–36; in Congress, 11; economic protest, 35; elements of, 36; eras of, 34; functions

of, 32; ideological, 35; independents, 36, 41; major, 32–33; minor, 33, 35; one-party system, 33; organization of, 36; presidential selection and, 74; single-issue, 35; splinter, 35; two-party system, 33–34
political socialization, 41, 47
poll, 48. *See also public opinion polls.*
poll tax, 39
polling places, 44
pollsters, 48
popular sovereignty, 24
population statistics, U.S., 9
postal powers, of Congress, 62
Postal Service, U.S., independent agency, 85
Preamble, 14, 24
precedent, 99
precincts, 36, 44
President, U.S., 71–75; in bureaucracy hierarchy, 82; as chief administrator, 71; as chief citizen, 71; as chief diplomat, 71, 79; as chief executive, 71, 77–78; as chief legislator, 71, 80; as chief of state, 71; as commander in chief, 71, 77, 79; election by House of Representatives, 73, 75; federal budget and, 83, 90; as head of political party, 71; nomination and election of, 73–74; powers of, 77–80; qualifications for, 71; roles of, 71; salary and benefits of, 71; selection process, 73; term of office of, 71
President of the Senate, 66
President *pro tempore*, of Senate, 66, 72
presidential election results, 10
presidential electors, 73. *See also electoral college system.*
presidential government, 15
presidential powers, amnesty, 80; appointing, 78, 84; commutation, 80; constitutional, 77–80; diplomatic, 79; executive, 77–78; executive

agreements, 79; executive orders, 78; foreign policy, 92; growth of, 77; how Presidents view, 77; increasing, 77; judicial, 80; legislative, 80; military, 79; ordinance, 78; pardon, 80; recognition, 79; removal, 78; reprieve, 80; treaty making, 79; war, 79

presidential succession, 72

primaries, kinds of, 43; presidential, 74; rules of, 74

prime minister, British, 118, 120

Privileges and Immunities Clause, 30

probable cause, 108

progressive tax, 88, 136

project grants, 29

proletariat, 123

propaganda, 53

property ownership, in free enterprise system, 122

property tax, 135

proprietary colonies, 18

prosecutor, 109

public affairs, 47, 51

public debt, definition of, 61, 89; interest payments on, 89

public health, State governments and, 134

public opinion, definition of, 47; leaders of, 47; mass media and, 47, 49; measurement of, 48; measurement through elections, 48; measurement through interest groups, 48; measurement through media, 48; measurement through personal contacts, 48; role of family in, 47; role of schools in, 47; shaping of, 47

public opinion polls, 48; scientific polling, 48; straw vote, 48

public policy, 51; interest groups and, 51

public safety, State governments and, 134

public-interest groups, 52

Puerto Rico, district court in, 98

punishment, capital, 110; cruel and unusual, 110

purge, in elections, 39

quorum, 22, 68

quota, 114

R

radio, 49

ratification, 20; debate over, 22

reapportionment, 56

recall, of governor, 128

recognition powers, of President, 79

referendum, process of, 127

refugee, definition of, 112

registration, voter. See voter registration.

regressive tax, 88, 135

representative government, 18

reprieve, by President, 80

Republican Party, U.S., 32, 34; domination 1860–1932, 34

reserved powers, 28

resolutions, congressional, 68; types of, 68

revenue sharing, 29

Rhode Island, ratification of Constitution, 19

rider, 68

rights. See civil rights; individual rights.

royal colonies, 18

runoff primary, 43

S

sales tax, 135

search and seizure, 108

search warrant, 107

Secretary of —. See department by name.

sedition, 104

segregation, 113

select committees, 67

Selective Service System (SSS), defense policy and, 93; draft for, 93

self-incrimination, 109

Senate, U.S., 55–58; approval of Cabinet members, 78; approval of federal appointments, 78; approval of treaties, 79; cloture, 69; debate in, 69; election of Vice President by, 64; filibuster in, 69; leaders of, 66; opening day in, 66; qualifications for membership in, 57. See also Congress, U.S.

senatorial courtesy, 26, 78

seniority rule, 66

separate-but-equal doctrine, 113

separation of powers, 24

sex, classification by, 112–113. See also women.

single-interest groups, 53

single-issue party, 35

single-member district, 33, 56

slander, 104

slavery, end of, 108; Three-Fifths Compromise, 21

Social Security. See Old-Age, Survivors, and Disability Insurance.

socialism, 123

sound bites, 49

sovereignty, definition of, 14

Soviet Union, cold war, 94; fall of, 119; government of, 119

Spanish-American War, 94

Speaker of the House of Representatives, 66

special courts, 97, 100

special districts, 133

speedy trial, 109

splinter party, 35

split-ticket voting, 36, 41

spoils system, 86

standing committees, congressional, 67

State, block grants to, 29; characteristics of, 14; compacts among, 30; constitutions of, 19; cooperation with Federal Government, 29; definition of, 14; extradition, 30; federal grants-in-aid, 29; Full Faith and Credit Clause, 30; new, 29; reserved powers of, 28; secretary of, 128; steps to becoming, 29. See also States by name.

State, Department of, 92; bureaucracy and, 84; secretary of, 92

State court system, 129–130; judge selection, 130; jurisdiction, 130; jury system, 129; kinds of, 130; kinds of laws of, 129

State of the Union address, 80

statutory law, 126

straight-ticket voting, 41

strict constructionists, 60; versus liberal, 60

subcommittee, congressional, 68

suffrage. See voting rights.

supply and demand, laws of, 16, 122

Supremacy Clause, 28

Supreme Court, U.S., 97–99; creation of, 97; decisions about freedom of religion, 103; federalism and, 28; how cases reach, 99; informal amendment of Constitution, 26; judicial review by, 99; jurisdiction of, 97; justices of, 6, 99; powers of, 28

symbolic speech, 104

T–U–V

Tax Court, U.S., 97, 100

taxes, assessment, 135; congressional power to, 61, 88; constitutional limits on power to tax, 88; corporate income, 88; custom duties, 88; direct, 61, 88; estate, 88, 135; excise, 88; federal spending, 6; gift, 88; income, 61, 88, 135; indirect, 61, 88; payroll, 88; progressive, 88, 135; property, 135; regressive, 88, 135; return, 88; sales, 135; social insurance, 88; socialism and, 124; State governments and, 135

television, 49

territorial courts, 100

Three-Fifths Compromise, 21

trade associations, 52

Transportation, Department of, bureaucracy and, 84

treason, 110

Treasurer, State, 128

Treasury, Department of the, bureaucracy and, 84

treaty powers, of President, 26, 79

trial, bench, 109, 130; by jury, 109; speedy and public, 109

trustee, congressional, 58

two-party system, 33; history of, 34

unconstitutionality, 24

uncontrollable spending, 90

unicameralism, 18; of State legislatures, 127

unitary government, 15

United Kingdom of Great Britain and Northern Ireland. See Great Britain.

United Nations (UN), 95; composition of, 95

urbanization, 134

verdict, 109

Veterans Affairs, Department of, bureaucracy and, 84

veto powers, of governor, 128; line-item, 80; of President, 24, 69, 80

Vice President, U.S., 72; as Acting President, 72; duties of, 72; importance of office, 72; as president of Senate, 66; election by Congress, 64; process of choosing, 73; succession to presidency, 72; vacancy in, 72

Vietnam War, 79, 94

Virgin Islands, specialized court, 100

Virginia, Mount Vernon Convention, 20; ratification of Constitution, 21–22

Virginia Plan, 21

voter behavior, nonvoting, 41; party identification, 41; psychological factors in, 41; social factors in, 41; split-ticket voting, 36, 41; straight-ticket voting, 41

voter registration, 39

voting rights, age and, 38–39; citizenship and residency requirements, 39; civil rights laws and, 38, 40; Constitution and, 38, 40; Fifteenth Amendment, 38, 40; literacy and, 39; poll tax and, 39; qualifications for, 39; registration, 39; U.S. history of, 38

W–X–Y–Z

war powers, of Congress, 62; of President, 79

War Powers Resolution, 79

ward, 36

Washington, D.C. *See District of Columbia.*

Washington, George, 22

weights and measures, standards of, 62

welfare state, 124

whips, congressional, 66

White House Office, 83

women, discrimination against, 112–113; equality before the law, 112–113

World War I, 93

World War II, 94–95, 118

Yeltsin, Boris, 124

zoning, 133